# Values Based Leaders in Action:

## *Over 125 Stories of Advice and Inspiration from Everyday Values Based Leaders*

**Edited by**
Chris Hitch, Beth Ritter, and Michael Saccavino

**Cover design by**
Madison Thompson

ISBN: 1544867395
ISBN-13: 978-1544867397

***General Shelton's Five Cornerstones of Values Based Leadership***

*Honesty*

*Integrity*

*Diversity*

*Compassion*

*Social Responsibility*

## *Dedication*

For Leah and all of the majestic creatures in her world-Hedgehogs and Simbas, Penny and Puffins, Squirrels and Apes, and Cats big and small.

**TABLE OF CONTENTS**

## *Foreword*

By General H. Hugh Shelton, USA (RET)

We have thousands of books on leadership written by academics and other leadership experts. Many of these books have leadership models or academic frameworks. We don't need another leadership framework. What's missing from all of these books are stories from every day people who strive to live an ethical life both personally and professionally. This book is a collection of stories of everyday people striving to do the right thing when they are confronted with making decisions to act ethically as a values based leader.

It is easy to lead others and manage yourself when things are going well. However, when you encounter ethical or moral dilemmas, you go through a leadership crucible where you are forced to come to grips with your values and their impact on others. We've always found that a values based leader is not necessarily a role, but the way a person behaves. The cornerstones of values based leadership-*honesty, integrity, compassion, diversity,* and *social responsibility*-define who you are as a person.

The stories you'll read have mostly positive outcomes, but there are some cautionary stories as well. These stories illustrate these cornerstones in many areas of everyday people's lives. We're confident they will inspire you to see how others have dealt with these ethical challenges.

## *Preface*

We have a fascination with shortcuts in our always connected, instantly on, world. We are always looking for ways to shorten or decrease the amount of time to do something. Sometimes we cut corners and the shortcuts give us some additional discretionary time. Frequently, however, we cut corners and it has a negative effect on us, those whom we care about deeply, and those with whom we work. You simply cannot cut corners when it comes to personal leadership.

This fascination with shortcuts may have started back in the 1990s when Bob Waterman and Tom Peters wrote the book In Search of Excellence. Many people say that book launched an entire category of books on business leadership. Peters and Waterman launched a business category that currently has about 11,000 books every year on leadership. The worst of these books follow a formula of "here's what I did. It worked. You should try the same thing. If you do that, you'll be successful."

It's more effective, in fact, to look at universal or generalizable characteristics from leaders that transcend a particular industry, profession, or career. After all, unless you are in the exact same industry, at the exact same time as the book author, you can be led astray. General H. Hugh Shelton is one of those individuals whose legacy and influence transcends any singular industry, profession, or stage of life. He has focused on five generalizable and universal cornerstones that he defines as values-based leadership.

General Shelton received a bachelor's degree in textiles from North Carolina State University and was commissioned as a second lieutenant in the infantry through the Reserve Officer Training Corps. He then spent the next 38 years in a variety of command and staff positions around the world. He served combat tours as a Special Operations Officer, was selected as an Army Ranger, and led multiple commands including the 82nd Airborne Division, the 18th Airborne Corps, and Commander of the Special Operations Command. He was promoted to a four star General.

General Shelton became the 14th chairman of the Joint Chiefs of Staff in 1997 and served two two-year terms. He was the principal military advisor for two United States presidents, President Clinton, and President George W. Bush. He was the senior military leader in the sky on that fateful day of September 11, 2001.

General Shelton retired from military service on September 30, 2001. During his career, General Shelton was decorated by 16 foreign governments, including being knighted by Queen Elizabeth II in 2001. For his exemplary service to this country, the 107th Congress bestowed the Congressional Gold medal on General Shelton on September 19, 2010.

His leadership extends to the corporate sector as well. His awards in the corporate sector include the Charlotte North Carolina World Affairs Council World Citizen Award for 2002, North Carolina's highest award for public-service, the Eisenhower award from the Business Executives for National Security (BENS), the American Academy of Achievements Golden Plate award, the Intrepid Freedom Award, and recognition as a National Father of the Year. He also has been named as a Watauga medal winner at North Carolina State University. General Shelton was also named as one of the top 100 corporate directors in the United States.

General Shelton has outlined five cornerstones of values-based leadership that apply to all of us, whether K-12 students, undergraduate or graduate students, early career professionals, mid-career leaders, and senior executives. These cornerstones are honesty, integrity, diversity, compassion, and social responsibility. It makes sense for us to take a look at what he has talked about, his methodology and cornerstones for success, and how they might be applied to our work rather than simply in one or two aspects of our business life.

Chris frequently heard him talk about how we need

more values based leaders at all levels, from high school students, to new college graduates entering their professional careers, to senior level executives. Working together, Chris and Beth asked students in their classes (BSBA and MBA) to go and interview some people they admired to see how these everyday heroes from different backgrounds, industries, and roles grappled with ethical dilemmas, how they ended up making those hard decisions, and what they learned from the experience. We ended up with over 700 hours of interviews through the hard work of the contributors listed in the back of the book. We had the difficult task to distill those 700 hours of interviews to the stories you have. These stories are their words. All names are pseudonyms and none of the editors know who told which vignette to the contributors.

This book is packed with real-life stories by everyday people who exemplified General H. Hugh Shelton's nationally recognized five cornerstones of values-based leadership:

- **Honesty:** telling the truth, even when it comes at great personal risk.
- **Integrity**: doing what you say you will do and demonstrating your values on a daily basis.
- **Compassion**: upholding your standards while offering empathy for those who struggle.
- **Diversity**: ensuring you get diversity of thought, experience, and backgrounds to bring together for positive results.

- **Social Responsibility**: focusing on a purpose greater than yourself.

You can see the list of all of the students who contributed to this project in the back of the book. They all did a tremendous job and we were heartened by the valuable lessons they took to heart from their efforts.

Values based leaders don't come with an exalted title. Instead, values based leaders exemplify the best we all have to offer. You'll see how these every day values based leaders apply these cornerstones when making hard decisions. These stories give us all inspiration that making the right decisions, using honesty, integrity, diversity, compassion, and social responsibility as cornerstones pays off, especially when it is difficult.

These are the stories from everyday values based leaders, told in their own words. All proceeds from the sale of this book go directly to the NC State University Shelton Leadership Center to help provide student scholarships for the Shelton Youth Challenge. We are confident that these students will be a part of the next generation of values based leaders.

## *Acknowledgements*

Thanks to General Hugh Shelton and his wife, Carolyn. General Shelton's story is well known and he is a singular example of the cornerstones of values based leadership. Carolyn Shelton, his wife, has been by his side since 1963. She is one of the most honorable people I've had the chance to know. She is a values based leader in her own right.

Thanks to the members of the Shelton Leadership Center Board of Advisors and the Shelton Leadership Center. Your unwavering dedication and passion for values based leadership is unsurpassed. My time at the Shelton Leadership Center allowed me to deepen my understanding of values based leadership and how one demonstrates those cornerstones in every interaction.

Thanks to Beth Ritter, my co-author, who also enjoyed encouraging her students to learn at the hands of many leaders. She and I partnered to bring you the best version of these interviews. Many thanks to all of the Poole College of Management BSBA undergraduate and MBA students. They helped illuminate the lessons of every day values based leaders. These anonymous leaders, who by their firm ethical foundation, help demonstrate that you don't have to cut corners and you don't have to be a pushover to be an ethical leader.

You'll find a list of all the contributors at the back of the book. These NCSU students from the Poole College of Management were tireless about interviewing and learning from whom they thought were values based leaders. One of the key points both Beth and Chris pushed was that one can be a values based leader, no matter their formal work role. Regrettably, we couldn't put all of the stories in this book (it would fill another book to do so). We are pleased that the contributors and interviewees demonstrated the NC State University motto of "*Think and Do*".

Thanks to the anonymous individuals who shared their candid stories about difficult decisions, and their willingness, through their stories, to "pay it forward". By sharing their stories, they've exemplified one of General Shelton's cornerstones of social responsibility. These individuals were courageous in sharing their stories. As we promised them, we sanitized all names to preserve anonymity. We are humbled and inspired by what they've taught all of us.

You never want to hire yourself as an editor. Thanks to Michael Saccavino, without whom this book would not have seen the light of day. Michael took the interviews and edited them for consistency and brevity. His quiet expertise, enthusiasm, and eye for detail made this book a much better read than if Beth or I had done it.

Thanks to Madison Thompson, our cover designer. Madison was able to take ideas that we had about the key elements of the cover (NC State colors and using the brick theme as a foundation for values based leadership) and transform them into reality. Her professionalism and expertise shines through.

Thanks to Helena Metot, whose keen eye for detail made this book better in many ways.

Finally, my utmost love and thanks to my family. April is my best friend and confidant, with whom I've had the great fortune to have had over 30 years in marriage. The best days of my life started when she said "Yes".

David, Rachel, and Leah- April and I look forward to seeing you grow your lives together.

Sarah-you have a tremendous passion and focus for helping those who most need responsible role models in this turbulent and chaotic world.

All five of you keep me grounded and make this corner of the universe a great place to be and serve.

All five of you are my most important values based leaders in action.

~ *Chris Hitch*

## *Career Changers: Some Choices Are Truly Career Defining Moments*

We saw a recurring theme in these interviews about career defining moments. Whether they were, in retrospect, career defining or not, is less important. Most importantly, to the person at that moment, the situation felt like it was a career defining moment. The pressure was intense. These high stakes created internal struggle and risk for themselves or for those working with them. In the following stories, you will see interesting word choices to illustrate the dilemma. Values based leaders made choices that often coincided with a short-term loss for a long-term gain. One said a "hurt today for the best tomorrow". You will see similar plots within different environments. Many take the risk and find that they and their career are not only but better, driven in large part from their values based decision.

## Make an Appointment

I was just recently promoted and in my new office with my door open when a junior level employee came in to introduce himself. Meanwhile, another staff member came walking into my office wearing a suit while the junior employee was wearing nothing more than overalls. Once the staff member walked in, in military standard, he dismissed the junior employee from my office. I immediately stepped in and told the staff member to hold on and that he needed to make an appointment to come back at a later time so the junior employee could stay and finish what he came to my office to cover. This was a significant event in my life and career because it demonstrated that I was able to make someone feel good and important who normally is not treated in such a manner.

I was raised to remember everyone has feelings and not to dismiss someone of a lower level simply because of their rank or dress. While others may have worried about damaging their career or offending the higher ranked person, there was never a doubt in my mind that I made the right decision. I showed the junior level employee that he mattered. I made the decision to turn away the other staff member and focus my attention solely on the gentleman who came to me first and from that point forward the men who were of junior level felt more comfortable approaching me. From such a little gesture, I created a relationship with that young man.

I learned that when you have the chance to walk the talk, do it. If you have the ability to influence another person, it has to be a positive influence. It is important to be consistent with your values and to be open with people about them. Being a compassionate leader matters and one needs to be compassionate to everyone.

## At a Crossroads Decision For Career Integrity

I am a financial advising representative at a major firm. My job is to advise clients and create financial security for them. I also take consultant jobs on a case by case basis. Around the office, I knew of sales representatives that were not doing business the right way, but were very successful within the company. I encountered the opportunity to make a big sale, but it would have required me to make some changes to the data and falsify information.

I was given a client that had spoken to a different representative within the office, but was now my responsibility. The client was initially quoted a price based on false information the other advisor had used to create that quote. While I wanted to make the sale and remain consistent with the initial quote, I was faced with the dilemma of falsifying information or potentially losing this client.

I decided to consult with a respected senior representative and explain the situation that I was in. After explaining the situation and asking whether or not to continue with the sale, I was surprised to hear he recommended that I continue to use the false data and make the sale as is with incorrect information.

I was confused and disappointed that someone that I looked up to as a role model in the firm was willing to compromise his integrity just to make a sale. My values and integrity are of the utmost importance, and I made the decision to call the potential client and let them know that we could not complete the sale unless the information was accurate. The client turned out to be understanding even though this increased their cost, and hired me anyway. They appreciated my honesty and felt more secure with my being their financial advisor knowing that I would hold true to my values and be honest.

This situation helped me to define my personal brand in business as honest and reputable, while my dishonest coworkers no longer work in the industry because of their bad reputations. I owe my career to my consistent integrity and I think values are the cornerstone of any successful person.

If I could share any advice with future business leaders, I would remind you that whatever you do on an everyday basis, make sure it is something that you can sleep with at night and be proud about upon reflection.

**FDA Slams Dishonest Doctor**

While working in a document review role for a clinical research organization, I identified inconsistency in one doctor's files as part of a pharmaceutical mega study. I was a contingent worker, but had significant previous work experience adhering to FDA guidelines. The inconsistencies I was seeing in these files warranted further investigation, and could significantly skew the data being used to get FDA approval and take the drug to market.

I had two options: take my concerns to the organizational leaders running the study, or contact the FDA. I chose the former, and repeatedly saw my concerns swept under the rug. I was told to keep my nose to the grindstone, that I wasn't there to bring up these concerns, and that visiting sites was an unnecessary and costly expense.

While I continued to voice my concerns to different leaders at the research company, the FDA independently performed a site visit to audit the doctor about whom I was concerned. The FDA came down hard and fast on the doctor and the research organization. The research company had to scramble to hire 20-30 contractors to frantically review all study documentation and fax all the study documentation to the FDA. At the same time, the company was required to perform immediate site investigations for every site and in a tight timeline, costing significantly more than it would have to do it "right" from the beginning. The doctor went to prison. The research company's reputation was ruined and had to eventually close down.

You know when you are doing the right thing, and when you are not. Choose to do the right thing. Guidelines are in place for a reason. It will cost so much more than the dollar when you don't "do the right thing".

## Teenager Learns to Not Judge a Person by His Title

During my high school years, I had a job at a local establishment. The boss of the establishment was having issues at home and it carried over to his work. He would show up late to work, smell like alcohol, and not perform his tasks well or in a timely manner. After a while, as I would close the establishment, he would tell me that a certain till or petty cash drawer would be short X number of dollars, but not to record the shortage. He remarked that it would rectify itself the next morning. Even though I was in my teens and thought that people of authority wouldn't steer me wrong, I knew something was fishy. It was significant in that it was the first time in my life a person who was supervising me had asked me to do something that I thought wasn't right.

If I didn't say anything and the shortage was discovered by my boss's boss or even another employee, I would be blamed for the shortage and thus suffer the consequences. If I said nothing, I could have said my boss asked me to do what I did. Even so, it still wouldn't have made it right. I reported this to another member of the management team who then told our district manager. Shortly thereafter, the boss of the establishment was fired as he was discovered to have stolen goods for his wife without paying for it. The new boss didn't ask for anyone on his staff to do anything unethical or dishonest.

I remained in my position and didn't have to deal with such a situation again. The boss in question was fired and blacklisted by a background check company that does checks for other businesses in the same industry. We all realized that money would be counted and reported only as we have it. The checks and balances put in place wouldn't allow any fudging of numbers at anyone's request.

I learned that just because someone is in a position above you, it does not necessarily mean all that they say or do is the correct thing. Sometimes your own common sense can be your best advisor and friend. No matter how a situation tears at you or poses a dilemma, your decision will not be called into question if you handle it with honesty and integrity.

## Background Check Mishap Causes Dilemma

As an account manager at a staffing firm, I was very happy whenever I landed a new client. Once however, I lost a client that I had worked very hard to obtain because of an ethical dilemma. New federal laws put in place in 2012 restricted our firm from making hiring decisions (for our clients) based on items found on background checks extending past seven years. This policy was relatively new to us at the time. After one of our recruiters verbally extended an offer to a candidate for a customer service representative job with the new client, that recruiter accidently ran a ten year background check instead of a seven year background check. This error was not caught and the ten year background check was sent to the client.

Approximately nine years prior to when the background check took place, past the federally mandated seven, the candidate was found to have committed a credit card fraud offense. Seeing this, our client refused to hire her for the customer service representative position. I pleaded with them but the CEO, who was a CPA, saw everything as if it were black and white and would not budge on his stance. I then turned to a partnering organization that handles our payroll and underwrites our risk. They told me that if the client didn't hire the candidate, we would not be complying with the law.

It was one of the most difficult things to do in my entire career but I dropped the client. Fortunately, we placed the candidate somewhere else but a large portion of potential business for our staffing firm was lost. Faced with the issue, I really thought there would be some way to resolve it but unfortunately there was only one route to take.

Looking back, I would not hesitate to do the same thing again. As a salesperson, this was the first time I had to fire a client. You must sacrifice now for the betterment and longevity of the company. You sometimes have to take something that hurts today for the best tomorrow.

## Be Honest about your Professional Past

I work for a company that seeks potential candidates on behalf of an employer. My primary task is to present the employer with highly-skilled candidates that they would be interested in hiring. I serve as the middleman between the employer and the candidate by narrowing the applicants and providing an unbiased perspective. Employers seeking my services are seeking highly qualified applicants to fill top ranking positions. The service I provide allows employers to request certain qualifications they wish the candidate to have in order to ensure that the potential candidates are selected ethically and unequivocally.

I was requested by a 50-million-dollar employer to find a candidate with legal experience to fulfill a CFO position within that company. I found a potential candidate who supposedly met the requirements that the company requested, which included previous work experience as a CFO for three employers. I presented this candidate to the company, and arranged a meeting with the potential candidate and the company CEO. The initial meeting was rescheduled due to inclement weather.

During the time between the initial meeting and the rescheduled meeting, the CEO of the company investigated the potential candidate, and discovered compromising information that the candidate failed to disclose. The candidate was a major party involved in a 20 year lawsuit that had reached as high as Supreme Court jurisdiction. The CEO immediately informed me of his findings, and to my surprise, I was not aware of this information.

With this new information, I contacted the potential candidate, and asked him to provide an explanation for these findings. He disclosed the details of the case, and explained that he had been involved with the wrong people which resulted in ten years of litigation to prove his innocence. This story was proven to be valid. However, when I presented this information to the CEO of the company, he had already labeled the potential candidate as dishonest.

The CEO explained to me that if the potential candidate had initially been honest about his past, he would have had a 50/50 chance of being selected for the position. The CEO now perceived the potential candidate as dishonest and untrustworthy. His dubious integrity, rather than his actual qualifications, prompted the company to reject him as an applicant.

I believe that the most valuable lesson I learned from this experience was the importance of due diligence. If I had properly researched the potential candidate in advance, I could have advised him to be honest with the company. By taking this approach, one may not receive his or her desired outcome. However, being dishonest leads to a continuous cycle which intensifies until it becomes impossible to recover. You will never regret living a life of honesty and integrity

## Boss Takes Credit of Subordinates

I was a supervisor at a local public service organization. The person I reported to (an associate director) was requiring me to do his projects for him since he was new to the organization and didn't understand the way things worked at this particular location. I did this for a while just thinking that it would make me a better employee, and I also figured it wouldn't last forever. I thought once he had been in the organization for a while he would have a better understanding of things and begin to do the work himself. However, he never got a handle on the job, and kept pushing his project work on me. As a result, the work I needed to accomplish sometimes took a backseat. Frequently, I needed to stay at work late into the evening, taking valuable time away from my family. In the beginning, I didn't feel that I had any options to resolve this situation, as he was my boss and I would have to go around him or over his head to solve the problem. I also didn't want to "get him in trouble." What made this and the end result harder for me was that I actually liked this director, and we did things like go to local baseball games together outside of work.

Eventually, I had been working so late, pulling so many hours, and doing so much extra work that I couldn't handle his responsibilities and mine. I went to one of the other associate directors and spoke with her about the situation and how I should handle it. She then spoke to the executive director for me, and I ended up having a private meeting with him. After showing proof of the work I had been doing, the executive director had a private meeting with the associate director and asked the associate director to leave the company.

The most significant thing I learned was that changing one bad situation has effects down the road that you cannot anticipate. However, you have to do what you can live with at that time. At that time, being away from my family, as well as not getting credit for doing work that was done at the expense of what I was supposed to be doing drove my decision. Getting credit for work isn't everything, but when that is the only thing you are doing, not getting any of the credit is something.

## Career Growth Through High Personal Values

Early in my career, I was a sales manager selling computer software. The company had great training and product marketing but the software was inadequate to support many of our customer's needs. Although the company developed a list of answers to common customer questions, there were many questions that could not be directly answered without risk of losing sales. Since I was not able to effectively answer the customer's questions, I began to ignore difficult questions. Many of my customers found my support lacking and began escalating to my management team. I could have easily provided inaccurate information about the software or deceived the customer about the software until they committed to engage with our company.

One afternoon my manager called me to his office to discuss the customer complaints. I highlighted that I had difficulties answering questions that would result in lost sales. As we discussed the issues, he highlighted that there are many ways to answer questions that would not have a negative impact. It is critical that you never lie to the customer and address their concerns in a professional manner.

Honesty about software challenges could lead to loss of sales, but building strong relationships with the customers would result in long term gains.

I realized that it was more important to remain honest and professional than to increase sales at the expense of personal dignity and reputation. Reflecting on this situation, I realized that my manager helped shape the way I see and address challenges. I could have easily been deceptive to gain more sales, but honesty and integrity help to shape my career. Short term gains are not worth your personal dignity. Living your life with high values will enable you to grow personally and professionally.

## Doing the Right Thing is Always Worth the Risk

As an HR director for corporate recruiting, my team had calculated a pay adjustment for over 100 employees based on pre-defined criteria. The president provided his interpretation of what I had presented and asked for clarification. He made a glaring error and my manager (a direct report to the president) immediately noticed the error and instructed me NOT to bring it to his attention. They were at odds with each other, and the intent was to make him look bad. The least that would happen is the president would have gone forward until someone else caught the error; worst case was the president would go through with the error causing pay issues and possible labor commission audits and fines.

I only saw two options: correct his misinterpretation, or not bring it to his attention as I was instructed (which to me really wasn't an option at all). So I went with the first option and corrected his misunderstanding.

I received backlash from my manager. I got an immediate email response stating, "this is not what I told you to do". Then the "punishments" began. My team and I (all salaried staff) were instructed that we must work every Saturday indefinitely. We had to send an email every hour from the office to prove we were on site. I got the cold shoulder, cryptic responses, and stabbing comments. After several weeks, we went back to business as usual.

I knew that I would be "punished" by my manager. My manager had reacted in this manner before with other perceived "lack of loyalty" situations. My biggest concern was losing my job. I also knew this would not be the last time I would be in this situation. If I didn't take a stand now, I'd have to eventually take a stand with a future situation. The dynamics were not going to change. Moreover, I believed the risks to employees and the company for the whim of an individual was too great. On a positive note, my manager "quit" several months after this incident after much pressure from the CEO (with whom she also had conflict).

I have my parents to thank for my values and strong work ethics. I wanted them to be proud; never disappointed. This was not a difficult decision for me. That's not to say that I didn't stress about the thought of getting fired! On the contrary, that fear was real and very concerning! Decisions of this magnitude are rare (thankfully) but there are small choices we make every day that have some amount of impact.

Bottom line: make yourself proud and don't disappoint yourself. The rest will "work itself out in the wash" as my mom used to say.

## Company's Culture Survives Ethics Test

A few years back, a few leaders within our organization uncovered that some of the teams in different regions around the world had discovered a way to close a case without generating a Customer Satisfaction (CSAT) follow up [ed. – A CSAT is a customer survey phone call that is scored on a scale from 1 to 5 for a small subset of customer support cases. These scores are an important metric for tracking our company's performance. Avoiding a CSAT for a customer case that went poorly would artificially inflate the overall average.] While this may seem like a minor issue on the surface, the metric that these customer satisfaction scores feed into is one of our most important metrics our company tracks.

It boiled down to two options: work with leadership to address the issue and correct the 'loophole' in the system, or keep quiet and take advantage of the situation. In reality and used sparingly, the impact would be minimal. If you have a customer that is angry for reasons beyond our control, you close the case where they do not get a survey. There was pressure by some in the leadership team to continue to close cases in that manner. We would sometimes see the regions taking advantage of the situation, where their scores jump dramatically in very short period of time.

The leadership team met and there was a strong push, to do the right thing and correct the issue. During our conversation, I said "you can walk me out of here for a lot of things, but you will not fire me over integrity and work ethic issues!" The situation was brought to light and the issue that allowed the survey not to be sent was corrected, with minimal fanfare. The teams (and leadership) that were exploiting the issue were made aware that this type of behavior was not part of our culture. This validated my personal beliefs that doing the right thing is not always easy, but is always the correct path in the end.

Remember that integrity and a strong work ethic are the backbone of a great company. Do not trade your values for a short-term benefit. You have to live with yourself and your actions!

## Courage Under Fire

There was a business error that occurred accidentally. In an attempt to fix the initial error, the person I had asked to resolve the issue made an even bigger error. This error breached a significant client contractual requirement. It was several weeks before I realized the error went against the contract. Once I did, I immediately went to my direct manager about the situation. Others involved in the issue pointed all fingers to me, as if it was a mistake that was mine alone, even though there were several people who had contributed to the error. The timing couldn't have been worse. A very high level and visible senior leader within my company was scheduled to visit our site within the next couple of days to meet the client partner.

With the upcoming senior leader visit looming, I could have delayed alerting people of the issue. My manager could have also chosen to hold onto the information about the error, and wait until after the senior leader had visited before she told the client about the issue. However, my manager made the courageous decision to inform our client of the problem prior to the senior leader visit. This inspired me to be honest and quick to let her know about the issue that I had uncovered and my role in it.

She offered me a lot of support during all of her discussions with her management. The client partner was very unhappy about the error but very impressed that we had told him about it with a very high profile visit waiting in the wings. Our client actually ended up working with us to figure out a solution that minimized the potential error's impact to our contractual relationship. The client also chose not to bring the situation to the attention of the senior leader who was visiting due to how my manager handled it. My manager lost respect for the others who pointed all of the fingers at me, and wouldn't accept any ownership for their role in the mistake.

I learned by coming forward very quickly when an issue was uncovered that the support was much stronger for me than it would have been if I had delayed informing people due to a high-profile visit. I also saw the courage that my manager had to continue pushing the information forward as well, despite the potential impact to her. I've had some recent experiences outside of work with a leader who is not acting with integrity and honesty. This negative leadership has brought complete disarray to the organization and the leadership team. The important work the team is supposed to be doing is not occurring as effectively as it should due to the loss of trust. This leader has also not taken accountability of errors that he has made, and has pointed fingers at others.

My lesson learned with leaders on both sides of the spectrum is that honesty always wins in the end. Even in a tough situation, when you are honest, it will make a better impression than dishonesty. It will also help you gain the support from people at other times when you may need it. My manager has been a great advocate of mine, and a couple of years later came to my aid unsolicited when life's problems impacted me.

## Work for a Company With Strong Morals

My boss was managing a "cost-plus" project for a large university where materials were being purchased from vendors. Cost-plus project means the more money spent on materials meant the more money earned for the company. This project coincided with my boss managing a project in his personal life where the same materials were being used. The boss awarded certain companies work based on the inclusion of materials for his personal use that was paid for by the university. These materials were further installed using company resources as well as the bosses' time as he spent less and less time on the actual project and more time on the personal one. This situation increased my workload substantially.

I went to a vice president to get help and was told, "to mind my own (expletive) business."

This gave me the impression that the vice president knew what was going on and was permitting it. At a convention a while later, I was talking to other industry workers who told me more stories about my bosses' unethical actions. A few other coworkers were present and heard the same information. I felt it was my responsibility to report the information during a year-end questionnaire.

The legal department contacted me immediately to ask further questions and conducted an internal investigation. The boss was fired a few days later. The company went further and paid for a 3rd party audit which fully disclosed the situation to the university. All costs were reconciled to ensure a positive client relationship.

Another vice president discussed the scenario and outcome with company employees and said he was upset that it went all the way to the legal department and that it should have been handled within their group. This speech came off as threatening and promoted a culture of unethical behavior and overall poor management. I left the company as soon as it was possible.

This story demonstrated that several individuals within this company division lacked honesty, integrity, and social responsibility. This lack of values contributed to the company culture in a significant way that decreased morale and overall productivity.

## Dishonest Employees at the Workplace

I work in HR, specifically handling employee payroll. I recently had an employee who was overpaid. The employee never said anything about the discrepancy to anybody within the company. Apparently, this issue was brought up from a recently conducted internal audit.

I had only one clear option: adjust the error and report the incident to my immediate supervisor. I sent an email to management notifying them of the error in the employee's timesheet. Things became somewhat awkward after I made the adjustment and informed my supervisor. When this issue was brought to the employee's attention, he refused to admit he had done anything wrong. After showing him the error and further explaining that future careless errors may cause bigger problems down the road, the employee corrected his actions.

People can be perceived to be dishonest because of fear of causing further damage. However, people will be more willing to listen and change if the situation is handled as a dialogue and a learning opportunity rather than a criticism. Try to always be honest in life and at work. Life is a full circle: what goes around comes around.

## Do What's Right-It Will Be OK

The agency I was working in decided to outsource a significant function that was previously handled in-house. The contract involved millions of dollars and the agency would lose about 300 jobs. The contract was written in a different office location, then it was handed off to my office to implement and administer the contract. It was a controversial decision to outsource and take away these 300 jobs and make them private. Upper management was determined that this was going to be a success since it was so controversial. Because upper management wanted it to succeed, there was a lot of pressure on us to make it succeed.

Unfortunately, the contract contained a lot of vague, ambiguous language. Much of the contract didn't explain execution so there was a lot of miscommunication on expectations because of the magnitude of the function and the poor quality of the contract. My upper management pressured us to re-write the contract to reduce performance requirements and increase the cost for the contractor. My upper management wanted us to work with the contractor to make sure it was successful.

One option was to do what upper management and the contractor wanted us to do; this was going against our best interest because upper management didn't want to deal with their failure. I had a co-decision maker in this situation. He was adamant about saying no and resist upper management. He didn't think the decision was ethical and didn't want to stand behind it. He would not leave any room for compromise since 300 jobs were lost due to this decision. He eventually was forced to retire because of his decision.

There were a hundred different decisions and interpretations made in this contract. We had to keep upper management apprised of what we were doing. I frequently met with our upper management to inform and consult with them to clean up the ambiguous contract language. There were definitely some gray areas and some areas to compromise. It was difficult to negotiate with the contractor because they knew our upper management was going to guarantee whatever they wanted. However, if the language of the contract was clear, we enforced it with certainty.

We went into negotiations and we came to some agreements but I was still dinging the contractor on areas where they weren't meeting the contract. The contractor wanted us to lower the standards and I couldn't in good conscience lower the standards; we put people out of work, we paid millions of dollars, and you want to lower standards? I'm not going to agree to that. My stance was, we want a performance improvement from what we had before, not worse.

The contract was eventually pulled out from my office and sent to another location where the people that ran the contract were much more willing to give the contractor what they wanted in the contracts. They gave a lot more to the contractor than I was willing to.

This was a 10 year contract-when that ten years was up it came back to our agency (in-house). The contract was horrible and it was never going to succeed.
For me, I don't think it hurt me professionally. Certainly, it affected the 300 people that lost their jobs. Some people retired and some people transferred to other locations.

My biggest lesson? I think it was a lesson in kind of keeping your head and working through each issue one at a time without emotion. It was a deeply personal and emotional issue about people's lives. It was a lesson in follow the logic, follow the regulations, try and keep emotion out of it, and take it a day at a time. It made me more confident as a person that I could stand up for what I believe. I tried to accommodate where I could, but I took a stand where there was no rational way of getting to where you needed to go. It was relatively early in my career but it gave me more confidence knowing that I could stand up to upper management with good reason and support my position.

My advice to others? It is worth keeping your integrity even if it does cost you, I think it can be done. In the end the contract didn't survive, but I think that more often than not that's the way it will fall out, it just takes time. You give where you can and you can still live with yourself. No job is worth living with something that you regret.

## Doctor's Office Employee Caught Red Handed by Manager Stealing from Company

While I was the office manager at a doctor's office I took over the book-keeping responsibilities. I realized that there was $30,000 missing from an account during a routine internal audit. An employee was stealing the money by filling out deposit slips incorrectly and pocketing cash. This went on for over a year before the employee was discovered.

I chose to go to the police to handle the situation. The guilty employee was terminated and arrested. He was convicted of a felony and ordered to repay money stolen through restitution. When the other employees were told about this they reacted with surprise and disdain. Their next reaction was to distance themselves from any money handling. They were all afraid to handle money because they didn't want to be accused of stealing. Policies had to be changed to protect employees as well as the business.

If you lose your honesty and self-esteem you lose your sense of being. Integrity is the most important thing I look for when hiring new employees. If you mess up, own up to your mistakes.

## A Young Career Put to the Test

I was young in my career, and dealing with a multimillion dollar transaction. The "options" in the transaction were heavily regulated. Someone who had been dealing with the options had botched the dates, and those dates needed to be correct in order for the company to make a lot of money. I was asked to back date them, which would be illegal and immoral in my opinion.

My only choices at this point were to either do what they asked, which I found morally wrong, or to say no and refuse to do it. However, I was unsure if I would get fired for not doing what they asked. I was a baby in my career field, and didn't have a clue. However, I knew you have to do what's right and do what you can to live with it in the end. To this day I would not go back and change the dates on the transaction.

I took a risk and refused to do the job because I thought it was unethical. The result was that management at the company said that was what they were expecting my answer to be, and it was ok. I was not reprimanded for the decision. This decision did impact others because after I said no, they ended up not changing the dates at all and losing that transaction. Maybe my actions made others realize how wrong it would be.

The significant lesson about this situation is that I learned that when I stood up for what I believed was right, other people followed. No one else in the company wanted to go back and change the dates either when I said no. Also, what I was most afraid of, getting fired for not doing the job, didn't even happen, so I made the right choice.

You have to live with yourself at the end of the day. That's what it really boils down to. You have to live with what you do or don't do.

## Company Fudges Numbers to Meet Goals

When I worked for a software company, sales had to get their orders in at the end of each month so that fulfillment could get the order shipped to the client and that the company could recognize the revenue. This became a more significant issue at the end of a quarter or end of year. On one occasion, I found that the fax machine date was changed and that the company also shipped blank software media to be able to recognize revenue if they were coming up short. This was usually done at year end when senior corporate leadership needed to make up for all the short falls of the prior 11 months.

I found this hard to believe, but as I got more involved with sales and the corporate employees that supported them, it was clear that they did not question what the CEO requested them to do. It appeared that they even turned a blind eye to it. Many of these were ethical issues to me, and I felt bad that employees were put in these positions. To me it is one thing for a person to be unethical but to ask someone else to contribute or potentially lose their job is a travesty. I, not knowing how it would feel to be put in that position, could not say I agreed or disagreed with them, I felt that I could not judge them as I was not in their situation.

I respected the CEO prior to finding out about this practice. His unethical behavior not only tarnished the respect that I had for him, but also those associates who chose to comply with the CEO's directive, without question.

As I grew in my position, I eventually was indirectly asked to do whatever was needed to exceed my target revenue number. The unethical hack had now become personal. I managed the professional services department, and we could only recognize the services that were delivered for each project. The company had a special program for clients where we were allowed to recognize revenue without having delivered the services.

I was confronted by the CEO, and was told I needed to do what I had to do to recognize as many service hours as possible. I told the CEO that I already do and he responded that he expected me to find every dollar that I could. It finally registered with me what he was asking; even if it meant falsely reporting revenue. I was so upset that I immediately went to my Supervisor, who was the General Manager for our division. I explained that I would not and could not fudge any contracts to meet a sales goal. He understood and said to just do my job and keep him informed about the status of meeting the sales forecast.

We would both confront the CEO if year-end business conditions could lead to unethical practices. Luckily, we were able to exceed our sales forecast through honest means. However, from that day forward I lost respect for the CEO.

Always make the ethical, value based career choices, even when it might seem wrong in the short term. For people faced with these decisions, you need to step back and say, what can we do to keep from having to compromise our core values (honesty, integrity, and compassion). I was fortunate that I had some great out of the box thinkers and many of them were excellent system developers. It is amazing how well associates can perform if you trust and give them an open canvas and ask them to solve a problem!

## Maintain Your Values and Beliefs

My boss was asked by the COO and senior vice president to change the findings of an investigative report of the company I worked for at the time. They felt it would have a negative effect on earnings. This situation was significant because it could eventually subject me to liability as I was involved in the investigation and creation of the report. To my knowledge, there were not many options available to resolve the issue. The way I understood it, it was either change the report, or don't change the report and face potential retribution from senior management.

Ultimately, we didn't change the report. The SVP resigned within the year, as their leg of the business was part of the report. The COO was cordial to my boss and the department after the incident. The COO ultimately came to respect my boss more as a result of the decision to not sacrifice the morals and beliefs that got them to where they were.

Given my profession, this was an important event to witness. Seeing the way my boss held strong in the face of such scrutiny, and the ultimate effect the report had on the well-being of the company showed that what I do is valuable, and despite what some may think, very much needed.

I have found that regardless of what some people think or say, having these qualities, and being honest about your faults will carry you much farther in life and in one's career than anything else. Always be true to yourself.

**Employee Commits Fraud over Medical Bill**

At a time when I was managing over 65 employees spread across two distinct business divisions, one of my direct reports exercised deeply unethical and unlawful behavior. The employee, who was responsible for the high risk function of processing payments, manually added a zero balance to a relative's account that had recently been a patron of the business and owed $500 for a service performed. The employee and relative had been given multiple opportunities to work with the business in developing a feasible payment plan. Instead, the employee committed fraud in an effort to prevent the relative from being turned over to collections. Another employee who witnessed the activity reported it to me and requested full anonymity and no further involvement in the incident. Although the amount owed was minimal, the dishonest and fraudulent behavior of the employee demanded a response.

I laid out three options for resolving the situation. The employee's actions could be ignored, I could directly confront the employee, requiring involvement from the coworker who had reported the incident and requested anonymity, or I could terminate the employee. However, the last option would be challenging without involvement from the "whistle blower" or any further supporting documentation.

Knowing that the right thing needed to be done, and that this would entail termination of the employee, I devised a strategy that would achieve this without compromising the anonymity of the coworker that reported the incident. This involved encouraging the "whistle blower" to contact and report the incident to the Compliance Hotline. This would ensure anonymity for the coworker, while also triggering an investigation into the fraudulent activity by Corporate Compliance.

The coworker obliged and called the compliance hotline anonymously to report the incident. In response, Corporate Compliance visited the facility and conducted a full investigation. The investigation confirmed the employee had written off a zero balance on the relative's account. The employee was then immediately terminated.

Reflecting on the ethical dilemma, I would like to stress the importance of following your gut and doing what is right, because employees look up to you and respect you for being honest and fair. Even though making the right decision may be uncomfortable, or may hurt others, it will pay off in the end. Had the incident not been reported, addressed and resolved, the implications to the business and its reputation could have been extremely damaging.

## Empty Stomach Saves Sourcing Professional's Career

In a previous job, a potential supplier gave me a gift card to a restaurant when I met him during the supplier presentation portion of a sourcing event for my client. Our company had policies in place to provide guidelines on accepting gifts and conflicts of interest. However, it is difficult not to think "how would anyone know if I accepted the gift card and used it?" Also, "I can still make an objective award decision regardless of whether or not I accept the gift card....I am not promising they will win the event." It would have (hopefully) remained just between me and the supplier, so it was a tough decision. I could have accepted (and used) the gift card and not told anyone, or I could have politely declined the gift card and advise that it is against company policy to accept gift cards because of my role.

I decided to tell the supplier I could not accept the gift as others could perceive I would be biased. I would also be at odds with our company policy to ensure a fair and objective supplier selection process. I also advised the potential supplier to not do something that could even possibly be perceived in a negative way because it would come back to hurt both of us.

He told me that accepting the gift didn't mean anything as far as the RFP was concerned. He wasn't expecting the gift to impact my decision, but it was merely to give me a warm introduction and give me an opportunity to try one of his favorite restaurants in Atlanta (I was from out of the area). I politely declined because I could not take the risk of being perceived as unethical. It was somewhat awkward throughout the rest of the RFP when I had to speak to him, but I was able to do my job without feeling favorable towards any RFP participant.

It was worth not taking the gift card even though I would have loved to try the restaurant. When we didn't select the vendor who offered the gift card, the vendor wanted to see all documentation from the sourcing event to ensure a fair process since they weren't awarded the business. If I had accepted the gift card then they did not win, I'm sure he would have used that against me to say something was done unfairly. It's certainly not worth compromising your values or career for a temporary reward.

## Listen to get the other side of the story

When I was working with a friend in my venture to a new start up, I was facing an issue of honesty with another partner. I wasn't completely sure what he was doing and some data were leaking out. We had to discuss the issue because I was becoming uncomfortable with the data flowing out of the system.

I thought I had to report this immediately but I wasn't sure whether he realized the impact of his decisions. After talking with my mentor, I decided to talk with my friend's business partner and hear out his side of the story before taking any action. My mentor had faced a situation similar to this before, when he was in a large corporation. He shared that he was on the receiving end of people jumping to conclusions. I wasn't sure what kind of issue he was referring to exactly, but he just mentioned it being a breach of conduct.

I felt really bad for him as I never thought that someone in his place could face a situation like that. He had been in the company for a while then and had a very good reputation with clients. He was not allowed to attend some meetings for a while. He was put into a committee where the breach was investigated. He had to go through them because he wanted to prove his side and I think he did it well.

As my mentor talked to me, I realized that the stakes were quite high for him personally and professionally. His job and professional reputation was at risk. He thankfully had proof to prove his point and his side of the story. It was clear that it was tough during the period when he wasn't allowed to attend meetings. As he was good with clients, we had to keep up with them until his return. But the committee was quick and he returned to the meetings very soon. Given his reputation and time in the company, he had a soft landing because people still gave him a chance to explain which he utilized very well to prove himself right. The committee members kind of apologized to him for bringing false allegations, but they had a different story to tell and so they settled.

As I listened to my mentor, it was clear that I needed to talk to the guy and give him another chance because he did not quite realize the impact of the leaky data flow from his perspective. We felt his side of the story was genuine. We had to be very cautious for a while because the trust was nearly broken, though I wouldn't say broken completely. We did give him a second chance but we had to take precautions and understand the implications.

I learned two lessons. First, be prepared for anything from anyone. Also, think through how long you will stand the difficult situation that is impacting you, your values, and the organization. If you ever face a situation where one person has not shown his integrity or compassion or honesty and has broken those values, give the person a chance to explain. I think this is especially important if you are in a small environment. For me, it turned out that he wasn't even aware of the fact that it was causing an issue and he maintained data security after the incident.

You should always be fully aware of what you do because people have different points of view and the same thing can be interpreted in two completely opposite ways. You do need to learn the other side of the story-you may be up for a surprise.

## The New Guy May Have Been Green, But He Wasn't Dirty

When I was in my twenties, I worked as an outside salesperson for a steel company. I took over my territory from an older salesman who had been in that territory for more than 20 years. Our company's customers loved this man, but, clearly, he had not worked hard for the past five years. Our company was glad when he elected to retire at 62. The man was very kind to me, and we traveled together for several weeks while he showed me the ropes. Many of the days we took a customer out to lunch and the older salesman would introduce me by saying, "This is John, he's young but he's sharp. He'll take good care of you." It wasn't long before I learned what he meant by that. Not more than two weeks into the job one of the customers called me in to say that he was planning to give me my first big order. "Remember though John. I take care of you and you take care of me." Obviously, he was fishing for more than steel. I left his office and called the retired salesman. "What exactly did he mean?" I asked. "Oh, John, he's a good guy, he doesn't expect a pay off, but it would go a long way if you dropped off a TV or stereo for Christmas, or golf clubs for his birthday. You just write off a few extra lunches here and there and you'll have what you need in no time."

I could have continued business as usual, written off the lunches and bought the expected gifts. Or I could use the change in personnel to change the status quo. I just sucked it up and decided to have the talk with all of the veteran's old customers. I told them how much I looked forward to doing business with them. I told them that I knew we could handle their business well with good products and great service. However, I was new on the road and I wanted to make sure that I kept my reputation and theirs untainted. "I sure hope to get to know you better. My company supports that effort and encourages good entertainment. Maybe you and your wife would like to go to a show and dinner with me and my wife, or our families could go to a ball game." I lost some business. However, I was in that territory for a number of years and at some point most of those customers had to give us another shot because the new company couldn't meet their needs.

The most important thing was that I knew that I got the business by being a good salesperson, and providing good products and great service. I would have always wondered how good I really was at my job if I had been giving out big gifts. I know I wouldn't have had the same confidence in my abilities. Eventually I got promoted back inside as a sales supervisor, the general manager of the plant, and ultimately the vice president of 13 plants, responsible for hundreds and hundreds of employees. You can bet that over the years there were times when employees bent the rules, or even laws. I was always able to say that from first-hand experience I knew it didn't have to be done that way. I also think that the confidence I got from facing that tough situation head on helped me feel that I could lead with integrity.

### *Extra Effort: The Right Choice Often Requires Extra Effort*

You'll read about the inconvenience and extra effort of doing the right thing in this next series of stories. Our interviews revealed that, frequently, often making a situation "right" was expensive, required over-time, daily intervention, or rework. One can see how that extra effort might discourage those that are not values based leaders. The rewards for the extra effort, however, included trust, improved partnerships, or just peace of mind of no further necessary rework. The adage of hard work being rewarded seemed to ring true for values based leaders.

## A Failed Marketing Campaign that Won The Trust

I was a brand-services executive with a leading advertising agency. One of my responsibilities was creating integrated marketing communications for a particular client. I vividly recollect my first encounter with a clash in opinion between my client's idea of an effective campaign versus our agency recommendation. Due to this conflict, my team developed three campaigns for the client.

Two of the campaigns linked with our recommendation and one campaign focused on the client's demand. During the client-agency presentation, we raised a red flag that their idea would fail to bring out the intended result. We also pointed out that it wouldn't make an impact in the already cluttered market making it difficult for customers to relate to the brand. The client however was adamant, so we agreed to have it their way.

Executing this campaign did not feel right. It was my duty to ensure effective branding strategies and advise my client on investing diligently for brand-promotions. I knew this campaign wouldn't achieve much and yet, I had to play along. I had two options. I could either go ahead with the client's demand without flinching or I could fight with the client in order to prove the agency's upper hand.

Either way, the campaign decision would tax the agency in some way or the other, as the agency would either be held responsible for the failure of the campaign or for being arrogant and difficult to work with.

During the client-agency presentation, I (I hope) raised a red flag that the client's idea would fail to bring out the intended result. I also mentioned it wouldn't make an impact in the already cluttered market. The client, however, was adamant, so our agency agreed to give in to the client.

I discussed my internal conflict with my managing director before the meeting. He appreciated my strong sense of ethics. He also patiently explained that this was an important client and they could not afford to make them unhappy. After all, the client is always right!

In our next meeting, I was apprehensive of reiterating the concerns for the risk of annoying the client. However, I decided to follow my principles and tried to convince the client to be open to the other routes presented earlier. The client ultimately chose to stick to their idea and our agency launched the campaign.

As I dreaded, the campaign wasn't well received by the target market and the client realized their mistake.

In my subsequent meeting, the client apologized to me for not trusting the agency's expertise and was impressed that I kept the best interests of their brand in mind. The managing director was also relieved since the responsibility of this failure did not lie with the agency, as we had raised our concerns with the client time and again. Our agency was able to maintain our reputation with the client, which was critical to our agency.

Lessons learned? I realized my ethics guided me all along and helped me juggle all ends. It taught me how to use discomfort as my signal to be courageous and a cue for action rather than inaction. I also learned that sometimes a mistake is the best way to help someone learn. Not only did the client value my integrity, but also learned to trust the agency more.

It is important to raise concerns in the right manner and at the right time. It also helps to explain the results of the situation. Clear communication is important to keep everyone in loop about the potential risks in an approach. You should never disregard your principles and work ethics.

## Bank Does the Right Thing with Federal Regulators

I was working in enterprise risk for a multinational bank. I was charged with creating a global risk analysis for the CEO to identify global systemic risks. My team worked diligently with consultants as we did not have the internal capability. We discovered a multi-billion dollar gap in controls upon researching a highly risky product. We knew we could conceal this from the regulators as another bank recently received a multi-million dollar fine for the same gap in controls. They did not disclose this and the regulators found out 3-5 years after the fact. I decided to take the issue to the chief data officer and the chief compliance officer with recommendations. We ultimately corrected the problem and looped in the regulators to share our action plans.

While we did not have ample time to remediate the immediate issue, we negotiated this issue with the regulators for the next iteration of the risk analysis. We began the journey to fix the gap. Fixing that gap was very expensive and, as always when a control is implemented, revenues are negatively affected. The organization rallied behind the effort after communicating the need for change. We successfully closed the gap and now have a stronger control against improper use of risky products at the bank.

I was initially surprised but I was impressed that personal courage exists in the executive management level. They made an ethical decision versus a revenue based decision. I got a chance to see ethics in action-it was quite powerful.

## Transparency is Key

I would like to share a situation where I think that honesty of the team was challenged and not just mine. Our team was being revamped after a couple of resignations, and the impression left on the client by one of the people who had resigned was not good. I had to complete a client deliverable and I was facing some minor issues, which I conveyed to the client. In turn, the client wanted to know what kind of issue I was facing even though it was a minor one.

I was sure that I would be able to deliver on time regardless, but the client wanted to be sure about the situation. I initially felt that the client was nitpicking, but then I realized that the client had every right to be critical of my work. This was significant as I was now the most senior member of the team after all the resignations, and how I dealt with this would affect the project.

I had the option of being reactive about the whole thing. This option would not have impacted me or my future prospects with the company. However, I chose to be proactive to gain the confidence/trust of the client. I decided to make the things transparent to the client no matter how small the issues or challenges were. I started having daily calls with the client just to keep him updated about all the issues I was facing.

Later on, I reduced the frequency to two calls a week after I had gained some of the client's confidence. As a result, the new team members were welcomed by the client on a positive note, and no one has faced this situation since then.

I learned a major lesson from this situation where I think the honesty of the team was challenged. It's better to keep the things transparent. This might be difficult to do in the beginning, but the long term positive effects far outweigh the issues faced initially.

**How Clean Are Your Pharmaceuticals?**

When I started my first professional job at a pharmaceutical company, no one trained me on what I needed to do. I didn't know there were production meetings I needed to attend in order to request things. Some months after getting into the job, I realized that testing had not been completed going from one product to another product (it's important to be sure you're not contaminating)—you need to be sure that the equipment is clean. I realized that this had not happened for a really difficult product to make.

I had a decision to make. I could do nothing and just start doing things correctly going forward or I could let the quality management know what had happened. I chose to let quality management know about the issue, and it was a big deal. It turns out that nothing had been contaminated, but the potential was there for retroactive recalls which could have cost millions of dollars.

I learned that most people come to work to do their jobs well and even when bad things are happening, people will roll up their sleeves and get it sorted out in the right way. You need to be able to live with yourself because jobs are fleeting but once you lose your integrity, it's gone forever.

## The Importance of Due Diligence Activities

I worked as a software consultant and project lead. My team decided to conduct a due diligence activity prior to releasing major software for a client. During our review, we found an issue in the application code. If this application code had gone to production, it would have caused production issues for our business partners and thousands of dollars in losses.

Being the development/technical lead, I decided to report the issue to the senior management and work on a defect deferral process. However, the development team was not happy with my decision and decided to not support me in the reporting process. Both the developmental team and my team knew that this could affect all our jobs if management did not take it well and choose not to accept the plan.

I developed a contingency plan and timeline to fix the issue. I then provided the contingency plan to senior management. Senior management approved the plan and we implemented the fix. They appreciated my team's due diligence and honesty in reporting the issue in a timely manner so as not to interrupt the business partners.

The end result was positive since our business partners were happy with the fix. They were not interrupted with any productivity, nor were they required to do any work correcting a potential defect. Senior management and the client appreciated our team for finding the issue. The client then included a due diligence activity as a process before every release. This helps to maintain a high quality delivery prior to moving the code to production.

The most significant thing that I learned was to report any issue to the management sooner rather than later, so we can proactively work on the contingency plan and help our business run smoothly. If I had hidden the issue from management, it would have turned into a big issue post production, losing thousands of dollars for the company.

Honesty will never let you down. Try to be less political and concentrate on quality and selfless service. Honesty helped us avoid a big penalty in this situation. Even though we initially had difficulties, everyone appreciated us for being honest, proactively reporting the issue, and providing a contingency plan.

## Benefits of the "Right Thing" Outweighs the Costs

While I was running my own business (a small marketing services firm), I was contracted to print brochures for a direct mail. My client had also contracted with a mailing house to handle the mailing of the brochure, so duties were separated between design production (my firm) and execution (mailing house). During the brochure design phase, I knew that there had to be space left on the final design so the post office could attach a bar code. This would grant a bulk rate to my client which amounted to a significant savings on the mailing.

I designed the brochure, left space for the bar code, and sent proofs to the client for approval. Upon approval of the design, we proceeded to printing and sent the final product to the client, invoiced the client, and received payment for our services. It was a big success for my budding company.

Some time later, after this project was closed in my mind, I received word from the client that the cost of the mailing for the brochure we designed was approximately $12,000 more than the anticipated cost. My initial reaction was to classify this as somebody else's problem since the mailing house was supposed to handle the mailing.

My part in the transaction was strictly design and print and we had approval on the design.

As it turns out the design did not leave enough room for the post office to print the barcode allowing for the bulk rate, so the client and the mailing house were considering it a design issue. Of all of the firms involved in this transaction, mine was the smallest, and could least afford to take a $12,000 hit unexpectedly. This amounted to approximately 2 months of payroll for my firm.

I had a few options regarding how to handle the situation. I could walk away and refuse to pay any of the additionally incurred cost. I had been paid and closed the job in my mind and on my books. As far as I was concerned, I had met my obligations and responsibilities in the deal. I could have taken the position that the mailing was the responsibility of the mailing house. They were the experts, and should have known what the specs were for the bar code and caught the deficiency. This was not my area of expertise, and I had no specs to go on for that piece of the design. The problem with this option was that I could see it would almost certainly lead me to a lawsuit in which I would have had to defend myself. I don't think it would be a problem to win, but I could definitely kiss any future business from that client goodbye. That was not something I was prepared to do.

Another option was to cover the $12,000 overage to make the client happy. On principle, I didn't feel like this was my responsibility. I truly did believe that my culpability in this situation was minimal, if at all. I didn't want to set a precedent that I would eat any errors in any project I was involved in. Also, my ability to cover this cost and recover as business was in serious question at the time. Lastly, I could call all parties to the table and negotiate a solution where everybody involved owned their part and felt that a fair just course of action could rectify this problem.

I decided the best course of action was to call parties involved to the table. For our part in it, we designed and printed a sticker which held the bulk rate bar code and could be placed on each brochure before sending in order to reduce the cost of the mailing. The client agreed to the "after-market" solution, even though it was not exactly in line with their brand. The after market solution took away from the look and feel of the marketing piece. The mailing house proceeded with mailing placing the stickers on the brochures and sending them out.

Everybody agreed that it was not a great situation for anyone, but it was the best we could come up with given the circumstances. Everybody said that they could live with this agreement and we implemented it. This experience cost me a good chunk of my reserves and changed the business services I offered going forward. It caused a lot of stress and aggravation for my firm and me. However, the client ended up happy and continued their relationship with me.

If you're going to do something for pay, be an expert at it. When I first started, I would do anything that someone would pay me for. If I didn't know what I was doing, I would buy a book on it, give myself a crash course, and figure it out enough to be able to pass off a job. From this point on, I figured out what my core competencies were and stuck to selling those. Not owning up to your responsibilities always feels worse than earning money unethically. Treating someone else the way you would want to be treated really should be at the forefront of your mind.

## Bringing Diversity Into a Male Dominated Team

As an IT development manager, I work in a predominantly male environment. Two years ago, I hired a new female software developer in my team. She was extremely skilled and effective. Hence, I promoted her in the end of the first year. However, her promotion stirred up conflict in my team because the other male employees do not like be managed by a female leader. The team also complained because she just stayed in this company for 1 year. The worse thing is that my company has not had a chance to conduct sensitivity training. Eventually, some of my male employees made inappropriate remarks to her. She complained to my boss and to me.

In response, my boss sanctioned those responsible for the conduct. Moreover, my boss tried to move the female employee to another position where she would be less likely to draw attention to appease the whole team. I strongly disagreed with this decision. As the department leader, I talked with my boss in order to keep the new female software developer in the old position because of her skilled ability was so important for my team projects. I thought this decision would be treated as a discriminatory problem. I also used my authority to talk with the male team members and try to show them her importance for our group and projects.

Meanwhile, I applied some budget dollars to build some type of team sensitivity training. Finally, I persuaded my boss and my members to keep her in the same position, and today, she has successfully led her team to finish many projects and earned a lot of money for the company. More importantly, she used her professional ability and positive attitude to demonstrate her personal and professional expertise to the whole company.

I took this chance to improve competitiveness of my team and to help my boss grow a new work environment. Now, the sensitivity training is a routine element of the regular training plan of our company.

## Always Take the High Road... Literally

We were paving a section of a highway outside of a major metropolitan area. We were behind schedule by a few weeks. Rain had delayed us, and the Federal inspector was pushing us to complete it by the end of the week. We came across a section that was not passing the quality control tests no matter where we were taking the readings. The inspector was pushing us to just find a new spot and call it good, rather than repave what we had done to meet the requirements. This is not usual, but in the overall scheme of the project really did not seem like a big deal. Since the inspector was willing to move ahead I was tempted to let them call it passing, but that was not the right thing to do. It could have caused serious problems and cost the taxpayers millions to repair in the near future if it was not done right.

I insisted that we take another look. The inspector was upset, but I assured him we would complete it on time. My crew was quite unhappy, but to this day we have not had a problem with that highway. After repaving, we were able to get the results needed to pass the section. We have not revisited that section to fix anything that was potentially done wrong.

It can seem really easy to take the easy route even when leadership is urging you to do so, but it never ends up that way. It is always better to do something right the first time no matter what.

## It's Never Too Late to Take Responsibility

Working as a project manager for the past five years made me realize that my decisions cannot please everyone at the same time. My team was always focused on delivering projects on time, and ready to work hard to keep project time a priority. However, I have to report a project slip if the job could not be completed on time. Reporting a project slip is a very tedious job. Project slips can affect other projects handled by my team and other teams. I decided to stay away from reporting a slip with one particular project, because I thought we could recover lost time. However, the situation worsened, and the slip was estimated to be nine months. This made me nervous.

I decided to report the project slip and personally take the blame. I also worked long hours to develop a project mitigation plan with my team, suppliers, and other involved parties, which improved the project efficiency. I had to leverage my relationships within the firm to get a perfect plan in place.

As expected, I received negative response from the top management. However, I was able to convince them about how hard we worked to create a fully effective mitigation plan, and how the plan could help avoid future losses in the project. In the end, the risk mitigation plan turned out to be a positive experience.

If you know something is going to happen ahead of time, it's better to address it then and there. Do not procrastinate such decisions. Understand that people appreciate it. It takes guts to report and take the blame on you.

## Do What is Right Instead of Following Orders

I have worked with an international consulting firm for a number of years. This extremely competitive industry meant a heavy work load. The office was continually concerned with signing up additional clients and new client development was a primary focus of the managers. I was taking the lead on selling a new client and getting that client under contract. After several client meetings, I came to understand the difficult task the client was requesting. I had serious concerns about whether our firm would be able to deliver on the client's demands. Not only was it a resource concern on our end, I also felt that the client was being unreasonable on the requirement timeline.

I had two main options with this challenging situation. I could either agree to the requirements as the client requested and deal with the situation as it developed, or I could come clean to the client and admit there were flaws with the current plan. I decided to bring the conflict up to my boss before making any decisions. I was worried about bringing the issue up to my boss, given the strong push within the company to sign up as many new clients as possible. At the meeting with my boss, he said pretty much what I thought he would say. He advised me to sell the services to the client and ignore my current concerns. He was fairly direct and made his intentions clear. After the meeting, I was very disturbed and upset at how the conversation had gone.

I did not truly know how I was going to handle the situation at the next meeting with the potential client. I was torn between the conflicting perspectives. At one point in the meeting, there was a lull. I couldn't help but speak up about my concerns. I told the others that, after doing research and further investigation and planning, I had concerns with the current plan. I stressed that I wanted to be open and honest with them. I stressed that an honest approach would be the only one they would get with me and that it would be key to ensuring success in the future.

The potential client seems caught off guard about my honesty. They calmly stated that they needed to adjourn the meeting for the time being and reassess our relationship. I was pretty nervous at the time about how the situation would play out. After I told my boss about what I had said, he was clearly upset although he managed to internalize it fairly well.

Two days later, the client called and requested a meeting. At that meeting, they wanted to personally thank me for my approach, up front honesty, and integrity. I was not expecting that they would respond that way but they did. There was no guarantee that the situation would turn out that way.

It seems cliché, but honesty is the best policy. I was so glad that I ended making up the decision I did, and everything turned out well. Since that time, I have been in situations where we lost the client due to honesty, but I have never regretted the decision to be honest.

## Ethical Issues in Humanitarian Aid

We provide free meals to kids in developing countries. Part of that process requires signing contracts with local agencies. These agencies then deliver the meals to schools. Some kids come to school only to get a free meal. Last year, one of the agents from our contracted partners in one developing country visited a school and found kids holding on to vouchers while waiting for their meals. He asked one of the kids who didn't have a voucher and he said he didn't have the money to buy one.

In another situation, our organization's free meals were found for sale in the markets of a second developing country. It was very disturbing since our partners sign a contract with us that states that they will not be selling the free meals. On the other hand, since we have so many partners in that country, we couldn't know which one had breached the contract.

In the first developing country, it was his call to decide how to proceed since we supply free meals to our contracted partner. He had the option to either give a warning to the school, or stop supplying them with free meals. The option to ignore was just not the right one.

In the second situation, we had the option to send more people to that country to investigate the matter further and trace back the meals found for sale to its supplier. We could also stop giving out meals. Alternately, we could to put tighter controls in place.

We decided to stop giving out meals to that particular school in the first developing country as it was a breach of contract. It was a very tough call, since some of the kids who came to school had no option for another meal. However, since he knows best about how things work where he works, I trusted his decision.

In the second developing country situation, we realized that sending people to Haiti for investigation would be very expensive for our organization and instead, we decided to put tighter controls on all of our partners in that country.

By taking away a contract with one of the schools in the first developing country, our partner set an example for others to follow. It was not an easy decision. The kids in that particular region were impacted. In the second developing country, all our suppliers were impacted by our new tighter controls. Our staff was also impacted as they had to come up with new agreements and setting accountability.

Be clear about what is important to you. Constantly, be willing to ask yourself whether your systems are in check with your values.

## Students get a Lesson in Integrity

I've served as Student Involvement Coordinator for a small private college. This role has afforded me the opportunity to serve as a mentor for many of my students. During my career, my actions have sent a loud and clear message about my personal values and belief systems. One instance sticks out in my mind where my integrity could have easily been called into question. I was tasked with purchasing gaming equipment for campus housing, but had to stay within a certain budget for an outing with several students. After selecting the equipment and games, I proceeded to check out. During this process, the students never left my side, and in fact offered suggestions as to what games to purchase.

After leaving the store, I could not help but think of how inexpensive all this equipment was. After reviewing my receipt, I noticed that I had only been charged for one of the two gaming systems. I immediately left dinner, went back to the store and notified management of the issue. After paying for the additional gaming systems and exceeding the budget, I was met with disbelief from my student who could not believe I would go through all of that trouble to correct a mistake made by the store. A situation that felt insignificant and required no thought, was, in reality, a very important lesson on integrity and honesty that I had never had intended to teach during this school outing.

In my mind there was only ever one option: go pay for the equipment. However, I could have easily ignored the discovery and never shared with anyone that the cashier had not rang in the second gaming system. After all, this was the store's mistake and not my own.

Aside from going over budget, the students learned a valuable lesson that simply because someone else made an honest mistake does not mean you should take advantage of it. I was disappointed that almost all of the students would have ignored the discovery and never paid for the gaming system. They all felt that it was not their responsibility to ensure everything was paid for before leaving the store. I shared with them that I would have not been able to live with myself if I had stolen the equipment and possibly caused that cashier to lose her job.

Personally, I realized that students are always watching and learning from your actions. For them, I hope my students realized the importance of acting with integrity even when it does not seem practical, and how their actions have far reaching consequences.

Your every action is being watched as a leader. You must always strive to live the life you preach, because if the two do not match your credibility becomes non-existent.

## Deciding between Right and Wrong

My father and I owned a pine straw business for nine years. We had contracts in multiple states. One of our contracts was in Florida. The contract usually lasted 6 weeks and took place twice a year. One of our employees, "Derek" (a pseudonym) traveled to Florida with our crews to manage the work being done. Derek was in Florida for about a week when we received a call claiming that the crew had almost finished one of the jobs. They spread a certain number of bales, and a certain type of pine straw. Immediately I knew that this was not the type of straw that should have been spread.

My father and I had several options: keep the wrong type of straw down, come clean with our customer, and bill for the straw that had been spread; don't come clean with our customer, and charge for the higher priced straw that was not spread; or fix the job before they knew about the error, and eat the extra labor and cost of product.

My father and I decided to fix the job before the error was discovered and eat the extra labor and cost of product. We quickly boarded a plane to Florida to run the crews and get the job done right. Derek had already returned home. When my father inquired about the problem, Derek confessed that he knew the straw was wrong, but he was ready to come home. We decided to terminate Derek due to this costly and careless mistake.

This decision put us behind on all of our other work in the area. We also lost an employee due to the situation and we didn't make as much profit having to pay for extra labor and product. However, there was no way we were going to be dishonest about this, so we never really waivered with our decision.

I think that living one's life focused on values that include honesty, integrity, compassion, diversity in all of its forms, and selfless service is the only way to live a truly full life. It is important to show these values as much as possible in our daily lives because we are being watched. Our children watch us, our peers watch us, our supervisors and other associates and acquaintances, all watch us. Living these values allows us to be our own person and set boundaries and standards for others to see.

## School Bus Fracas

I had just begun a job as a principal at a magnet elementary school where kids have to apply in order to be accepted into a competitive program for gifted and talented students. One of the parents on the interview committee was one of my biggest supporters. He was very involved with the school and had been at the school for seven years. Several months later, his child was punched in the head by another student on the bus. This was a major safety concern to students, the bus driver, and others in the vicinity. The aggressive student responded by saying, "I didn't mean to hit her that hard." The parent of the victim asked me for the parents to settle the difference outside of the school without official documentation or reporting.

I could have complied with the parent's request, but it went against my ethics. It would have put other students at risk. Bus riding is a privilege, not a right. If you break any school rules, you can lose your privilege to ride the bus. I replied by saying that the distraction is a safety concern, and would have to be handled consistent with the school policies in place. The parent was not pleased and he quickly withdrew his support for me. His actions and resultant verbal retaliation caused substantial political strife.

Micro-politics can ruin any situation but there are pivotal moments in life that define you. All you have in life is your integrity and when you rest your head at night-you need be able to sleep with a clear conscience. Your values are all you have. I want be judged and remembered for my character. A true leader must have strong values and always act in accordance with them.

## We Could Have Gotten Away With It (But We Chose Not To)

During a technology project, my team members and I came across a glitch in one of the programs. To put things into context, this glitch was something done abroad. In a few days, we would be out of the country and this glitch wouldn't be noticed for quite some time afterwards. The company had millions of dollars invested in the program's success. However, we also had to consider our company and team reputation with our decision.

We could ignore the problem and probably never get in trouble. We could raise the issue with management so that they fix it in the future (find a way to fix it, bye!). Finally, we could fix the problem ourselves. I decided our reputation and integrity was on the line, as well as the possible effects this would have on the client's business. We pulled one last "all-nighter" and fixed the issue. This was the right call because management recognized our hard work and the client appreciated our concern for them in the future.

I learned that when you raise the issue of integrity and reputation, people are willing to put in the extra work. Always do what you feel is right, in the long run your good deeds speak louder than your words. Actions are powerful, especially if they convey integrity.

## Firm Confesses Error and Makes Things Right

A project manager in my consulting company was working on a large consulting project for a major metropolis in the southeastern United States. At this time, he passed duplicated work to another project in another state. This action was not allowed and restricted by the contract.

When senior management found out, they met to decide what to do. It was extremely unlikely that anyone outside the company would find out that the work was duplicated and used on a separate project. The firm could have easily swept this under the rug and felt confident that it would not come to light. The other option was to volunteer the information to the major metropolis and hope they respected the intentionality.

The senior leadership looked at the company's foundations and core values. Ethical decision making was a key component, and they knew they had to volunteer the breach of contract to the metropolis. I felt proud to be a part of a firm that would do the right thing even if it was painful. I admired how they looked at the big picture instead of taking the easy way out.

When the senior leaders of the metropolis found out they were extremely upset. Even though we volunteered the information, the metropolitan leaders refused to make another payment until the problem was resolved in their eyes. It took years to restore the relationship and the company lost a significant amount of money.

Profits are important, but not as important as doing things right. Going over budget is not as important as doing right by the client.

## *The Golden Rule: Treat People Like You Want To Be Treated*

We frequently hear words of advice like, "Do the right thing when no one will know it", "Listen to your inner voice for the right answer", or "Only honesty and transparency matter". You'll read stories in this section of different situations, yet, all apply variations of the Golden Rule. You'll see how these everyday values based leaders demonstrate their values for those whom they lead.

## Lack of Integrity Results in Bad Choices

I was working in logistics, and a team member was selling raw materials for money on the side. This significantly affected our team's chemistry and our company's bottom line. The company initiated a comprehensive internal investigation to find the culprit. I had the option to try and cover for my team member or honestly cooperate with the internal investigation through data transparency and interviews.

I complied fully with the investigators and I chose to be transparent and honest. The guilty team member eventually admitted wrongdoing and lost his job. After this incident, it made me realize that engaging in non-ethical behavior could negatively affect your job, future, and personal life. It will always catch up to you. Always do your best to be honest and do the right thing. If you exhibit the opposite behavior, it will be your demise. My grandfather always told me, "Your word is all you have." You discredit your character when people can't trust what you say. If people can't believe in you or trust what you say, your words become irrelevant.

## Gold Necklace Saved by Gutter Cleaners

I own a lawn care company. One day, we were cleaning the gutters at a house and my employee found a gold necklace on the sidewalk in front of our client's home. He could have kept it and never said anything, or he could report to the homeowner that we found it. We decided to return the necklace. It was the right thing to do. The homeowner said she had been missing it for a week or so, and she was very grateful to get it back. This situation demonstrated my employees have integrity and business ethics. They can be trusted in or at anyone's home.

The client was really happy and grateful to get her necklace back, and we gained a customer for life. I was really glad to see that my employee did the right thing. I always tell them that we are operating a business with integrity. They aren't the richest people in the world, and finding a gold necklace could be a nice windfall. However, my employees know how much integrity matters to me, and they didn't think about keeping it for even a second. Make sure your employees are aware of your values because they are a reflection of you and your business.

## Administrators Applauded for Strong Stance Against Reckless Behavior

I work for a university, and I had to make a decision that would greatly test my ethics. Some members of a prominent student organization made some bad choices that resulted in the serious injury of another student. The investigation moved swiftly and uncovered evidence that would result in significant punishment for the entire organization.

This situation involved many stakeholders of the university, including students that had only one semester remaining before graduation. My decision would impact all the remaining members of the organization, along with the organizations alumni. The university's administrators had a lot at stake as well.

The situation quickly turned political, as influential alumni got involved to salvage the organization. I ultimately had to make the decision on the punishment. I faced everything from bribes to threat, but I stood my ground and delivered the punishment that I felt was appropriate.

This situation was significant, because handing down a severe punishment was not only deserved, but would also send a strong message to other organizations which would help us begin to change the culture of the university.

I had several options at the time. I could have swept a lot of my findings from the investigation under the rug and avoided the political backlash. I could have given into threats, or taken the bribes that were offered to reduce the punishment. I ultimately did what I felt was the right thing to do, even though it ended an organization with a long history on our campus. The decision was supported by my superiors all the way to the top of the organization.

I learned that you will always have those that disagree with you about the decisions and choices that you make. However, at the end of the day, you must make decisions based on your beliefs and values.

## Hold Your Business Partners to High Standards

Several years ago, a revered local small business vendor and my company found ourselves in a tough spot. Their higher than average product cost was due to the expense of our production standards and the expense of yearly audits. It had been our mission and my personal passion for several years to grow the local business. We informed customers about the product and supported it, and eventually, the vendor grew a large demand for their product. We increased our orders over time to the point that the vendor also started to grow its business to support us. In the midst of their growth, they made some questionable decisions that put a strain on our working relationship.

I had a duty to the stores who bought the product, to the customers, to the local vendor, to the stockholders, and to myself to make sure we stayed true to our word on the product quality. I only saw one option that was honest: address the situation with the vendor, knowing it would cause an issue for all those involved, and probably end up with us parting ways.

When I found out that the vendor had cut corners to keep up with our demand and earn as much revenue as possible, I had to make the decision to refuse the current and future orders and sever the relationship until another audit could be performed at their expense. This was not a pleasant experience. Everyone was upset. Customers wanted the product they had grown to love. Stores wanted the sales dollars and happy customers. The vendor wanted to continue making money. Some people wanted the issue to have been swept under the rug. I had many uncomfortable conversations with upset people. The vendor lost our company's approved status and we had to work on finding a replacement. I tried to set it up for the vendor to return after another audit, but they felt hurt by the way some colleagues treated them, and I was unable to patch up the relationship.

Always do the right thing. It is usually much clearer than you realize. Doing the right thing can lead to uncomfortable situations and conversations, lost revenue and profits, and many other undesirable outcomes. It also is the best way to sleep at night and have a chance at retaining loyal customers in a highly competitive marketplace. At the end of the day, you can always go home with your honor. You can always feel good about the way you treated others. You can choose to appreciate all things as a blessing or a lesson.

## Be Candid and Always Tell the Truth

I am a director at a major software company. At the time, I had a big commitment with a two-million-dollar revenue mark. However, the General Manager over-estimated the development effort as 80% complete, when in reality it was only about 60% complete. This project's success or failure was extremely important to me. Its' success or failure would impact my credibility at the company.

I had two options: keep my mouth shut and respect the General Manager, or tell the truth and reset expectations. I chose the latter. I voiced my concern to the GM privately after the meeting, suggesting that he was being too optimistic about the situation. The project suffered a slight delay, but it hit the market as a well-polished product, and it met the target revenue.

Through this experience, I learned that transparency trumps everything. The most important thing is being honest, and everything else will follow. You will not get very far in a large organization if your goal is only to survive. Only honesty and transparency can build your character. Your credibility relies on those two things and nothing else. This is the most important thing in your life as well as your career.

**Be Honest about Feedback to your Team**

Management asked for my feedback about a contractor our team had hired for one of our critical assignments. The contractor had been with us for a few weeks, but was unable to cope up with our requirements and demands. I could see he was trying hard, but in the end, I had to be honest about my feedbacks and not let my team down. The only other option I had was to say nothing and let things go on as they were.

I took the larger picture into account, and informed the management about the shortcomings of the contractor and his inability to meet the contract requirements. My feedback (backed with facts and figures) was taken seriously, which led to the contract termination.

It turned out that my decision was appropriate. My team began a rigorous search for a new replacement, which we soon found. Moreover, the management was even more cautious in the selection process to ensure the contractors held the appropriate credentials. This became a source of relief for our entire team as finding a suitable person helped us meet our deadline and provide the optimal service to our client.

I learned that it is always best to be honest about your feedback. My frank and open feedback not only helped my team and me, but also helped build a trustworthy relationship with the management. It showed management I had respect for not only them but for the contractor as well. It also saved some contractor anxiety from this assignment.

Always be true and fair to yourself and to others. At first something may not feel or look good, but that choice will always be appropriate if it has been made with honesty.

## Do The Right Thing Even When It Is The Hard Thing

I was working in a leadership position at a struggling manufacturing facility. The factory produced high-quality products, but was behind its corporate metrics for revenue and on-time delivery to customers. I had been repeatedly advised by senior management to do everything possible to hit our third quarter numbers. My team and I worked long hours in September to try to end the quarter on target in both revenue and on-time delivery. At the end of the last day of the month, production finished their final order, and the quality team began their inspection before shipment. A quality technician approached me and nervously shared that he had found a defect in the product that could lead to a customer safety issue. There was not enough time left in the day to rework the error. I had to decide between shipping defective product to a customer and calling corporate to let them know that I had failed this critical assignment.

Despite the immense pressure from corporate, I told my team and my team leader, "John", that the product had to be reworked to fix the defect before shipment. Expecting the worst, I immediately contacted management and informed them of the situation and my decision.

The head manager's response was that he was disappointed in John and would have to consider replacing him. John returned to his team with encouraging words, letting them know that they were doing the right thing by fixing the defect before sending the product to the customer. They worked late into the night correcting the error. The product shipped the next day, solidifying the miss on revenue and on-time delivery for the quarter.

Later that day, I received a call from the senior management team. Rather than fire me, the head manager apologized for his comments the previous day and thanked me for doing the right thing. He told me, "Metrics are important, but nothing is more important than providing our customers with safe product." In the end, I kept my job and actually exceeded fourth quarter metrics to close out the year successfully.

My key takeaway from the experience was to always follow my moral compass. I could have impressed corporate by making my numbers that day, but I wasn't okay with a customer getting poor quality product that could potentially cause injury. A lot was at stake, but to me, doing the right thing was more important than making my bosses happy. When it comes to living one's life focused on values, my advice is to never succumb to pressure to take shortcuts or the easy way out.

## Integrity: Not Just a Buzzword

When I was a manager at my last company, I was faced with a difficult technical problem which could impact the company financially to the tune of millions of dollars. Silence fell upon the room when the leadership team assembled for a meeting to determine a course of action. Nobody had any ideas, but we needed to make a decision. Acting as the technical conscience for the organization, a young manager made a recommendation which had the potential to cost the company millions in lost revenue, but ultimately was the prudent thing to do. The leadership team rallied around the decision, and proceeded to take action. The young manager in question could have provided guidance contrary to their values and saved the company money in the short run. Regardless of financial consequence they made the difficult decision, when others would not.

The decision ultimately led to short term losses, but potentially saved the company far greater losses if they chose to continue without resolving the issue. Clearly this was a difficult decision, but it reflected the value of integrity that was central to this particular manager's value system.

The most significant learning from this was to never fear tough decisions if you know they are the right thing to do. Act with integrity, follow through, and be consistent. This particular decision raised this manager's credibility in the eyes of the entire organization because they knew he would act with integrity in the face of adversity.

The most valuable lesson shared with respect to values based leadership, is to stay true to yourself, even if individuals you lead don't always agree with your decisions. If you are consistent and predictable, you will build trust. Always provide a consistent message, and back it up with action.

## Beware of Accepting Improper Benefits

I had a very close friend who worked for a city's Chamber of Commerce. While talking about the recent membership drive, he mentioned a noticeable benefit given to one of my colleagues for getting a lot of memberships. At first, I did not think much about it, and chalked it up to my friend being funny. Within a few days, my friend contacted me with the intent of telling me about another suspicious benefit given to the same colleague. At this time, I realized my friend was not kidding about the first conversation. Moreover, several other people were noticing the same thing. It was drawing negative attention to the company, and the acceptance of gifts from the Chamber of Commerce was unethical. I won't mention the exact benefits received, but I will mention that there was a lease of a luxury car and a cash bonus.

I knew it was time for us to do something. After pondering and realizing we must intervene somehow, I recommended that my friend bring up the benefits to our colleague's manager. After that conversation, an investigation was started and although our colleague was not fired, I heard that he had to return all gifts and was "very thoroughly coached".

This experience always makes me think twice about things that could be borderline unethical. Listen to your inner voice. It's not always about the noise and influences going on around you, but trust your original gut instinct.

## Quietly Leading by Example

One of the senior leaders at the company I worked for could not return to the office due to weather before his approved time off ended. Therefore, he technically should have been charged an extra two days. It was my job to charge the leave. However, as the senior leader he could have deemed that his situation was different and he did not need to be charged. There really would not be any repercussions except for the fact that this was not the most ethical answer. The truth of the situation was that no one would know that he was not charged for the extra days except for him and me.

He could have just not mentioned the issue, which would mean to not charge him the extra days. He could have actively said not to charge it ensuring that his intent was clear. Lastly, he could have made sure his extra time was indeed charged in order to be 100% ethical.

The senior leader sought out our section and made it entirely clear that he wanted his extra time properly charged. He even noted that he knew that no one besides us would know that he chose this route, but he wanted to make sure that he was treated the same way as the least senior person in the organization. His time off was then charged and nothing more was heard about the situation.

The situation resolved itself uneventfully. No one talked of it. However, I respected him so much more. It says a lot about someone who does the right thing when no one will know it and when doing the wrong thing would not have any real effects.

## Company Rises to the Occasion For A Greater Good

I owned a consulting company back in 2001. This company had about $2 to $3 million in revenue, and employed about 20 to 30 people. Right after 9/11, the resources began drying up. The situation called for a layoff of around 30% to 50% of staff because 90% expenses were human capital. My choices were to either cut resources, layoff some employees, or reduce salary of all employees.

I decided to cut salary across the board, and open discussion within the company. I was being transparent as an owner, and tightening the belt on the company's expenses. Surprisingly, my employees stayed on board for the good of the company. Because of the decision to cut salary rather than lay off employees, I was able to save jobs and increase employee loyalty.

Don't be afraid to talk with people when you don't know how they will react. Always be open and honest with people.

## Corners Aren't Meant To Be Cut

One situation where I faced an issue of honesty or integrity is when I had the opportunity to take advantage of someone in court. The situation involved foreclosure of a deed of trust with a borrower. I had two options. One was to do the right thing and continue the matter for another day. I also had the opportunity to basically cut some corners and get it over with as soon as possible and move on. I called my boss and filled him in on the situation and told him that we were going to continue the matter. He was ok with that solution. Everything ended up being fine. There was some impact for more time and expense involved with the case but ultimately it was the right thing to do.

The most important thing I learned was that while it is important, money is not everything. For example, I do not want to be known as the guy who will do anything for money, such as bending the rules a little bit here and there. I want to be known as an honest and hardworking person; one that is always known for doing the right thing. I believe that money will come. Your name and reputation means more than a quick dollar. It is longer lasting.

## Integrity Wins Again

I recall one significant situation with a part of a team that negotiated a national agreement which affected 240,000 people. Once finalized, people were assigned to go back to individual companies to reach an agreement on vacation allotment, percentage pay raise, etc. Negotiations with a specific company occurred thereafter. That company (ABC) wanted an improvement in benefit packages. They had $12,500 worth of life insurance provided to each employee at no cost to the employees. This type of insurance did not require employees to pass a physical.

ABC's management and union then reached an agreement and increased life insurance to $25,000. Contract drafts were reviewed, which consisted of documents of over 100 typed pages. People were assigned 7 or 8 pages to go over in detail before signing off in agreement. The company was required to print the agreement into a booklet, but made a 3-ring binder in case they wanted to change a page or two.

When the agreement came out, he asked the same people to compare the new and old contracts as a double check. They found that instead of that small increase, the employer misunderstood and increased it by $25,000, which made it a grand total of $37,500 worth of life insurance. Two members of their team said they did not want to say anything about the mistake. However, as team leader, I said "We are going to tell them about the mistake and we are going to agree to fix this." The VP of Labor relations for the firm did not know about it, and his people had not caught it. The union negotiator knew ethics was the reason he brought it to his attention, even though they could have gotten away with it. In this situation, in my opinion, I felt there was only one option.

In addition to the increase, ABC wanted something else, they wanted the national agreement to include a clause that the employee must have a checking account and within 12 months the employee must have direct deposit set up to draft into their account. They worked with the companies and agreed to accept direct deposit if they could keep the additional $12,500 making it $37,500. "Win-win situations are what it is all about in relationships!"

Honesty is the best policy because that is the only policy that is sustainable. A lie is eventually going to be discovered. We judge ourselves by our "best" intentions and we might judge other people by intentions only, so give the other person the benefit of the doubt.

## Expedience vs. Integrity

In 2006, I was working for a small software company. We were developing some custom additions to our product for an extremely large insurance company. The president of our division oversaw me as project manager. During internal testing, we noticed a significant bug in the code. The customer had not discovered the issue and probably would not until sometime after the delivery date. Making the delivery date meant that we would be able to realize a significant amount of revenue in the current fiscal year, but if the problem was discovered by the customer, it would damage our relationship and put future work in jeopardy.

We could have delivered the product with the bug in it and hoped that it was not discovered until after we had time to fix it in a future release. Alternately, we could tell the customer what we had found and indicate that the delivery date would slip. There was a lot of argument between me and the development manager, but the president intervened and challenged the development manager with a simple question "Are you willing to bet your entire year's bonus on the fact that we can fix this bug before it impacts the customer?" The development manager relented; we informed the customer and fixed the bug. We missed the delivery date, but maintained a good relationship with the customer.

It can be difficult for people to own their mistakes. Sometimes people are more willing to gamble with the reputation of the company than they are with their own compensation. People need to understand that decisions made at every level can make or break a small company.

## Dentist Saves Friend from Drug Addiction

I worked as a dentist at a dental clinic. One day, the pharmacist called me and informed me that one of my patients was at the store and had a prescription for a very large quantity of a pain medication that I prescribed to the patient. The pharmacist wanted to confirm with me the details of the script, to ensure that the script was valid in terms of dosage, quantity and directions. The patient was a good friend of mine and I faced a troubling decision of what to do in this situation.

1. I could verify the prescription with my staff
2. I could call the patient and speak with them
3. Cancel the script and decide whether to reissue

I decided to cancel the script and called the patient to return to my office to discuss the situation.

We discussed the call I received from the pharmacist and the large discrepancy between my script and what the pharmacist received. I asked the patient what was going on to learn more about the discrepancy. I found out that the patient had become addicted to pain medications. I recommended that the patient talk to their family and provided a rehabilitation brochure. The patient recovered after going to rehab and we remained friends. He is still a patient of my clinic today.

I learned that not everyone can be easily trusted when dispensing controlled substances. I learned that controlled substances are very easily abused and the pharmacy is good at spotting red flags when it comes to scripts from the dentist. I should work more closely with my pharmacist and started utilizing e-prescribing when applicable. You form close relationships with your patients in order to build a strong network of trust. However, it is a bit of a paradox. You also have to be cautious about even friends taking advantage of your kindness in the situation.

## Don't Make Do, Make Right

At my prior employer, I worked in a manufacturing plant that employed a diverse group of individuals. A significant (25%) proportion of our production population was Hispanic, and could not speak, read, or write English. These employees made significant contributions to our company, however, I had many challenges communicating with this group since I wasn't bilingual and neither were they. Over time, I began to wonder, "Did they truly understand what was being covered or discussed during company huddles or production communication meetings"?

We tried a few things to alleviate this barrier between the English- and Spanish- speaking population. First, we had a bilingual employee conduct a second presentation meeting with Hispanic employees directly after the original meeting concluded. This worked to an extent, however as I observed, I realized this only further separated this group from the rest of the production team. This directly contrasted with our desire to have a united workforce – the Hispanic employees did not get to hear directly from leadership, a benefit extended to other employees.

We then tried to include all employees in every meeting by having a staff member translate each slide after it was read aloud in English. This did not work well – it extended the meeting time significantly and made the overall experience for everyone involved less enjoyable. I began to think, "What can we do, but more importantly, what *should* we do?" Our business model was centered on "the greater good". We had a responsibility to look after our customers, and just as important, our employees.

I then remembered our company had once used an interpreter simultaneously during a company-wide event so that both English- and Spanish-speaking listeners could understand. This service worked by giving headphones to Spanish-speaking employees to wear throughout the meeting. While the speaker was presenting, a translator standing in the back was able to translate the information into Spanish almost simultaneously. The Spanish-speaking employees were able to hear this translation immediately through their headphones. I began to think, "How awesome would it be to include this service on a more frequent basis to improve communication with the Hispanic population of employees?"

I conducted research and put together a proposal that included the approximate cost per year for this service, as well as the cost of the equipment that would be needed. I shared the proposal with the Vice President of HR, who then shared it with the Executive Leadership team. After review, we quickly implemented this proposal. We realized this was an opportunity to show the value we placed on all of our employees. Additionally, this greatly benefited those who otherwise would continue to feel left out of the communication process.

The time and money spent on this proposal was money well spent. I immediately saw the interpreter's impact had during our first team meeting. During the presentation, Hispanic employees were able to follow along with the slides, nod their heads in understanding, and share in the laughter when jokes were told. Although the implementation of this project created additional work for myself, the overall benefit exponentially outweighed the cost. This small act made our work environment more united and inclusive and showed that our company was willing to embrace the diversity within and take action on a situation before it became too large of a problem.

Looking back, I learned that if you see something that isn't working well, do something to improve it – don't be afraid to challenge the normal way of doing things. Management and the Hispanic employees were content with the first two options. Don't be afraid to address an issue where others perceived there to be none. This proposal resulted in a more successful and cohesive workforce. Sometimes we have to put ourselves in the shoes of others and ask, "How would I feel if I were one of these employees?" I knew I would want to see the importance of my participation in all company activities in a way that was inclusive of the entire workforce. I believe this perspective should be kept in mind when leadership in any organization is making decisions and working to improve their business.

## Honesty Is The Best Policy

As a small business owner, I am faced with many decisions each day that can positively or negatively affect my business. One example occurred when I remounted an heirloom diamond provided by my customer. While tightening the prongs, I chipped off the corner of the diamond. I could fix this mistake in a couple of ways. I could have replaced the diamond with the same size and quality and let the customer continue to think he was presenting his grandmother's diamond to his fiancé. Alternatively, I could tell the customer of the accident and work with him on an amiable solution.

There was really only one option in my mind. I had to be honest with the customer. Although he was very unhappy that his grandmother's diamond was broken, he did not want to reduce the size of the diamond that he was presenting to his fiancé by having his grandmother's diamond re-cut. I obtained several diamonds of similar size and quality as his grandmother's diamond and allowed the customer to pick a replacement.

While the customer was very disappointed that he was not able to present his fiancé with his grandmother's diamond, he was satisfied that I was open, honest and acted with the highest degree of integrity. As a result, I was able to keep this customer and sold him the wedding bands for his wedding a few months later.

Accidents happen. How you manage these situations allow you to grow. Your reputation as a fair and honest business owner is vital to a small business success.

## Help Others Do the Right Thing

In college, I discovered that one of my classmates was just flat out copying material from sources for a research assignment. This was right before the internet made this practice discoverable with a search of the document, so this wasn't necessarily something that would be easily caught. Of course, the whole situation is an exercise in dishonesty, but it's also sort of a wasted opportunity for you to learn from the work you should be doing. Beyond that, I was also doing this assignment and making sacrifices to put in the research and time editing to do it right.

I had the option of turning him into the administration for a breach of the honor code. This would be within our school's acceptable culture as everyone (I thought) considered the honor code to be a core value of our college. I could also just talk to him and call him out. Who knows how that would go? I wasn't interested in reporting people's behavior like we were in grade school. I know that would have been the "legal" way to do it.

Knowing about this plagiarism was a burden that made me consider my own ethics where silence could be considered consent. I recognized that I wasn't exactly going to be the cool kid by going this route, but I decided to talk to the him and tell him that it was really despicable for him to be dialing in the assignment and pulling material straight from the book when the rest of our class, including me, was working hard to make the best of a tough assignment. Talk about a stick in the mud.

It turned out that he admitted to me that he was cutting corners on the assignment and pulling the material out. He told me that he was overwhelmed and just figured he could survive the course going that route. He acknowledged that it was wrong, just that he felt cornered. I offered, despite being swamped myself, to help him in taking some of the material he was copying and to revise it, internalize it, put it into his own words, and cite it. He got an extension on the assignment with points deducted, but ended up passing the assignment. Obviously, this was a way better option than getting expelled. Be willing to stand up for the right thing, and to deal directly with the people involved.

**Young Woman Stands Up to Older Men**

I work at an airport as the resident project representative. I am in charge of communicating with the contractor and airport representatives, inspecting materials prior to installation, and interpreting construction plans. While working on a tree clearing project, storm drains and underdrains were being installed in the airport. Before installing storm pipes, I am in charge of inspecting them for cracks and defects. There were several storm pipes which I identified as unsuitable before being installed. After I identified the unsuitable pipes, the contractor project superintendent suggested that I act like I did not see the pipes so they could proceed.

Although it seemed like a small issue at the time, this was my first experience working in the field and it was important that I maintain authority.

The answer was obvious: we would replace the damaged pipes. At the time, I was a 22-year-old female in charge of several older men. Contradicting them and giving instruction to replace the pipes was not particularly appealing. Although the pipes would be in the ground and it was unlikely that anyone from my office or the airport would find out about the damaged pipes, I instructed the contractor to replace them. Although he was annoyed, the contractor agreed and had new pipes delivered to the site.

My advice would be to always do what your gut says. When I'm faced with a difficult decision, the right thing to do is usually very obvious. Actually, doing it is the challenge.

## Ethics Is About How You Treat People

We provided a bid to a potential customer who capitalized on their size and influence to squeeze us hard on pricing. The customer informed us that they wanted to buy our product, but that we'd need to bid through an integrator that they'd selected to manage all their vendors. We provided our pricing to the customer during the direct bid, but this information was ultimately used to our disadvantage. After deployment, the entire experience was a nightmare. The customer did not realize the value they had hoped to gain by having an integrator as the "single throat to choke." The customer then secretly approached us directly to negotiate cutting the integrator out of the deal.

This was significant because agreeing to the customer's request would mean improved profits, less frustration/distraction, and a return to our standard business model. However, this decision would also mean violating our corporate ethics. All members of our leadership team were involved in the decision process.

We ended up with two options after our internal leadership meetings. We could either agree to the customer request and cut the integrator out of the deal or decline the customer's request. The leadership team quickly decided to decline the customer's request. I admired the speed and consensus of our team to decide to decline the customer's request. We all felt that it was in conflict with our corporate ethics and simply not how we should treat other people.

Ethics is personal and it's about how you treat other people without being artificially motivated to do so by financial or legal obligations. Given the pain and challenges with the integrator, we probably could have justified cutting out the integrator by claiming a breach of contract or some other technicality. We all agreed that it wasn't the right way to treat other people.

Ultimately, our company was extremely successful. Our business strategy revolved around work ethics and moral ethics. We felt that if we worked hard and honestly then we'd prevail. Within an 18-month time period, we increased our company's value by a multiple of 8 which was a direct result of a sound strategy, hard work, and ethical business practices.

Lessons learned? It's something a previous manager shared with me early in my career and continues to be meaningful. Success is based on 50% hard work, 40% ethics, and 10% other forces. Always be honest.

All ethics come down to the individual. You hope to promote synergies in a group, but it's a personal choice. Unfortunately, bad things happen. When you work hard and do the right thing, you can feel confident. Businesses are transient, but it's how you treat others that has a lasting effect.

## Age Discrimination in Hiring

I had a situation while working as a Talent Acquisition Manager for a major finance company where one of my clients, an internal hiring manager, was overtly practicing age discrimination during one of his hiring decisions. This was significant, as it is not only a direct breach of company policy, but it is also illegal.

My options were simple. First, I could do as I would do in most circumstances and make the client happy by doing as he or she had asked. Or second, I could have a frank discussion with the hiring manager explaining why we could not make hiring decisions based on the candidate's age. Furthermore, I would have to inform the hiring manager that I would have to report him to the appropriate HR channel if he insisted on eliminating the candidate from consideration based on age,

Even though it was tough and it would be easier at that moment to just be quiet and appease the client, I decided to have the frank yet hard discussion with the hiring manager. At first, the hiring manager still refused to interview the well-qualified older candidate. So, true to my word, I reported the incident to the proper HR channels. They, in turn, forced him to at least interview the candidate before he made a hiring decision. The well-qualified older candidate interviewed very well, and was shortly thereafter hired into the company.

The lesson learned is that doing the right thing is usually not the easy thing; however, in the end, it feels good and good things will come of it. One should always try (in life and business) to treat people and situations with integrity and compassion as one would want to be treated.

## Honesty and Integrity Can be Tough Lessons to Learn

I was recently hired to manage an animal feed warehouse. It was known that inventory was disappearing. Everyone suspected someone was taking inventory and selling it as a way to make extra money. The warehouse was on a small island in the West Indies. The local population was about 40,000 people. There are few employers on this island and the institution that ran this warehouse was one of the largest and most sought after employers of the local population.

I knew if I found an employee stealing inventory and fired him, his future employment opportunities on the island would be limited for quite some time. Theft is not ok. However, firing a local employee may have a large impact on not only that individual, but that individual's family and security for years to come.

The employee who was stealing inventory was identified. I attempted to eliminate this behavior by giving him a thorough understanding of what would happen should he get caught again. Ultimately, he was caught again and fired.

I was afraid. I was a foreigner and fired a local from one of the best employers on the island. In my off time, I volunteered at a local auto shop who worked to train young people how to work on cars. After a few months, the fired employee joined the training program and I had the opportunity to assist him in learning a new trade. It was uncomfortable at first, but ultimately we had an opportunity to develop a different kind of relationship based on mutual respect, honesty, and hard work.

I feel I may have been able to handle things differently. I might have fired him sooner than I should have considering the long-term consequences of that action. However, I'm confident that individual had an opportunity to develop his personal values. I often think of what he may be up to and worry he has trouble feeding his family. However, I'm confident that my actions, while maybe not optimal, were correct and justified. It can be difficult to live life with a set values system. It takes continuous effort to maintain and develop those values further.

## If You Work with Data and Facts, Why Would You Not Be Fully Transparent?

While working for a previous employer, I was involved in a contract negotiation between the union and my company. We were negotiating over the company's health insurance plan. The company's current health insurance plan projected to rise by almost four times more than what the company currently paid. This would have meant a much larger expense for the company that they could not afford.

In the negotiation, the company offered the union a whole new plan which was a less generous plan for the employees, but it was something the company could afford to pay. The company had two options when they presented the plan: they could either say it was a whole new plan and it would still be a great benefit, or they could be open and honest and explain that the company really couldn't afford the current plan at new rates and would have to cut costs by using this new and less impressive plan.

The company decided to be honest and open with the union, which was the best possible choice because the union was very open to cutting benefits if it meant that they could help keep the company profitable. After all, if the company was losing money they would have to get rid of employees. I was grateful to witness how that company operated with honesty throughout the negotiation. Openness and honesty are a great way to enter a negotiation and make the best decision for all involved.

As part of the negotiating team, I had the possibility of cherry-picking the data that I could have shown to the union. However, I chose to show all of the data, and in being transparent, they were more open and honest with the union than the law required. In the end, the union and the management both agreed to accept this new plan, which was more affordable for the company.

## Insurance Fraud Leads to Schools Closing

I work with commercial insurance for schools. I had a relatively new account with an area school and the insurance quote covered both the school and the school's founder's car. After about one month of having insurance, the school went financially insolvent. The founder called me and asked me if he could keep the car insured under the school's account. I explained to him that it would not be possible considering the school's closing. The founder argued that they still needed the auto policy since the school's leadership was still running strong. I found out later that the founder could not get personal auto insurance due to his driving record. He was attempting to commit insurance fraud to maintain the "school's" car.

I was left with two options. I could either issue him a new business auto policy, or I could cancel his insurance and leave him without anything. The only true reason he wanted a new policy was because of his terrible personal driving record. He simply could not afford to have a car under his name. Under the business policy, the driving record would not be pulled, and the car insurance rates would be significantly less.

I chose to cancel the contract, because it was the only ethical thing to do. I risked him bad mouthing me to other schools in the area, but it was the right thing to do. After the policy was cancelled, the founder was vocally disappointed with my decision. He was left without insurance, so he could not drive. I believe he got another agent to write him a policy, but I am pretty sure that agent had no clue what he was getting involved with.

Always do the right thing. This decision may have cost me a couple of relationships, but doing the right thing always dominates, even with the short term risk of losing some business relationships.

**Insurance Company Protects the Innocent by Settling Fairly**

I've spent my entire career in the insurance industry. I started out in the claims department and I'm currently a regional sales manager. As a seasoned claims adjuster, I handled cases with large liability. I typically deal with cases where coverage was difficult to discern and included multiple layers of coverage across numerous insurance platforms and policies.

One case involved a young man over the age of 18 but still living with his father. The young man was involved in a significant motor vehicle accident. The young man pulled out into traffic and collided with another motorist. The police report found the young man at fault and both parties were badly injured. My company had issued the car insurance policy for the young man and his father. The ethical dilemma from this case involved whether or not we would include the parent's policy to cover the excess damages. During the coverage investigation, the victim's attorney asked probing questions about the policy but did not directly ask if the parent's policy could be included in the claim.

My duty is to protect the insurance company and settle the case fairly. In my opinion, my options were to either settle the claim with only the young man's policy which would have a low pay out to the victim and possibly risk further litigation or to include the father's policy while settling well within a reasonable limit.

I felt that it was in my company's, my client's, and the injured party's best interests to include the additional policy. This decision increased the amount paid to the injured party but it also reduced the risk of further litigation which would be well beyond the amount paid. Also, I felt that it was the right thing to do to take care of the injured and protect the client and her company from litigation. The case was settled with no additional actions. I continued as a successful claim adjuster until I moved into sales management.

Lessons learned? It is best not to make quick decisions. I needed to fully understand all parties involved concerns and what they stood to gain or lose from the investigation. Importantly, I also sought counsel from our legal department and other senior claim adjusters. I also had to ensure my decision aligned with my values of personal integrity.

Your name and personal integrity are the only things in life that you own. Hold them in high regard.

## International Researchers Account For What Counts

I was tasked with hiring crewmembers from a developing country to work on a six-week international research project. The budget was extremely limited, and the crewmembers would have taken any wages offered, given the economy of the country. I had almost full autonomy over the budget. I wrestled with some significant questions. With autonomy over the budget, I could hire the crewmembers at the country's minimum wage (USD $9.70/day), I could allocate money elsewhere to much-needed equipment, or a larger crew with less pay, or I could increase pay and spend most of the budget on better wages.

I decided to go with better wages, paying double the minimum wage for inexperienced crewmembers and triple the minimum wage for experienced crewmembers. Despite having to hire fewer crewmembers, the project was completed and turned out extremely successful. The crewmembers were very happy with the wages, and worked extremely hard for them, even given the fact that I paid them in full upfront. Morale was high, and people felt valued rather than quietly exploited.

When I look back on this experience, I reflected on several different related challenges. When dealing with people's livelihood, I decided to truly understand the local living wage and then pay for quality. I learned that quality outpaces quantity and that quality pays off in the long run. I could have easily completed the project with lower wages, but at what cost? We were already extracting data from the country with no long-term commitments. We needed to do something positive in return. The crewmembers benefited from the project more than anticipated, which directly extended to the happiness and well-being of their respective households. Our decision increased the value they placed in themselves and their work.

People often say to learn from your mistakes – I would say don't make them in the first place. More often than not, there is an obvious honest answer among a body of options out there. Sure, I have no stockholders to answer to in my research, but I do have stakeholders, as do most projects and businesses. When it comes to impacting a life, a household, or a community through your decision-making, ask yourself, "What am I taking, and what am I leaving." I try to look to Epicurus with ethical dilemmas, "Happiness is the ultimate goal in decision-making, and to maximize happiness, minimize harm ... not for a subset, but all involved. That, in part, will always be the measure of success surrounding the research, the individual, the company."

## Office Politics vs. Doing What is Right

A few years ago, I was a manager at a technology-based company. The company had a somewhat innovative product they released which held a lot of promise. This product came with a number of contracts and terms. The company decided they would be extremely transparent in regards to explaining them to the public. However, after a year or so, the company began to realize that there were some "revenue" issues with the terms they had initially provided. Luckily for them, there was a clause within their terms and conditions stating that certain usage rights or abilities could be limited at any point at the company's discretion. While serving as lead project manager, I learned that the company was looking to implement this clause, essentially without notifying the consumers.

I saw this as an ethical issue, as well as an unsound business practice. To block this decision, I had to sway the opinions of key employees. The most significant thing that stood out to me was that this decision quickly became a popularity contest. Simply saying "this is what the company has always stood for and operated on" (i.e. rationality and vision), would not necessarily win people to my side. I had to determine how I could win people over to my point of view.

I held numerous meetings in plain sight of upper management with like-minded co-workers regarding alternatives to usage restrictions, mainly to show that it simply wasn't just me thinking this way. Regardless of how it was achieved, I was finally allowed to sit in on key decision-making meetings, and ultimately quelled the enactment of the clause.

In the short-term, these tactics were successful. However, it's worth noting that in the long run (after I had left the company) the clause would later be enacted, much to the dismay of customers. It's hard to say whether my ethical stand made an impact and times simply changed, or if my efforts simply delayed the inevitable of a company with its mind already made. Regardless, I can sleep easy at night knowing that I did what was right.

## Is A Temporary Gratification Worth A Tarnished Reflection?

In a former job, a supplier gave out AMEX gift checks as holiday gifts when onsite for a weekly meeting. Receiving gifts, at the time, was not against company policy. However, receiving "cash" or its equivalent has never sat well with me. Other group members also received the same type of gift and, for a brief moment it did make me think, "who would know?" It also made me think about if accepting such a gift influenced me in continuing to use this supplier's services. I mean, this gift card was quite generous. The decision was not easy.

As the supplier had left for the day and I did not get to open the gift until later that afternoon, I technically had accepted the gift. My options then became to either quietly use the gift, or raise it to the level of the department head.

I decided the ethical decision was to raise it to the department head and turn in the gift. Immediately I alerted the supplier, and requested no further acts of generosity as it could tarnish both my and his company's reputation.

The supplier was a bit taken aback and contended that it was a "thank you" for the large amount of business provided during the prior year. It was "common practice" to be generous with clients who supported his company.

It wasn't meant to feel obligated for future work – "although future work is always welcomed". I said I understood and thanked him for the generosity and politely declined keeping the gift by letting him know it was now with our department head.

The department head came to realize this supplier made his way through the department and offered up similar gifts. Word had gotten around I had declined the gift and turned it in – which created some ill feelings with other team members (who I guess felt entitled to the generosity). At the end of the day, I felt confident with my decision, actions taken and my ability to make supplier decisions in the best interest of my company rather than feeling "obligated" to the supplier who provided this gift.

If I had to do it all over again, the only thing I would do differently was not accept the gift to begin with. Even though the gift could have gone to many uses, I feel, as did the department head, the right call was made. One needs to look at themselves every day in the mirror. Is temporary gratification worth a tarnished reflection?

## The Majority Doesn't Always Win

I manage several people in my company. One of my direct reports was beginning to make a trend out of arriving to work later than normal. He provided seemingly honest excuses to explain his behavior. His responses initially gave me no reason to pursue further action. This employee had a very impressive work ethic and professional track record so I didn't think there was anything going on that was worth worrying about. I took him at his word, documented the late arrivals, and continued on my way.

At the time, I simply believed what he was telling me without suspecting that there could be anything more to the story. I later learned his late arrivals had been caused because he was attending interviews with other companies. When I initially presented this information to the supervisors in our work center, they all wanted to fire him without any type of concrete evidence of wrong doing and without scheduling to meet with him in person about the situation. I struggled with this recommendation without talking with him first. I scheduled a meeting with him so that I could find out exactly what was going on before we made any final decisions.

I spoke with the individual and asked him what was going on. It turned out that he was searching for employment elsewhere because he had just learned that his wife was pregnant with their first child. He believed that he needed to seek out a position at another company in order to obtain a salary that would accommodate raising a child. As a father of two, I was instantly able to empathize with him. He is much younger than I am and I believed that was a contributing factor to his lack of understanding of how his actions and being dishonest could negatively impact his career. I explained how he should approach our management team about requesting a raise, especially since he has been such a high performer. I knew that we would rather pay him a little more rather than let him leave.

After we talked, he followed my advice and was able to negotiate a raise. He also apologized to me and to the management team for his actions and their effect on the team's morale. Initially, there were some people in the work center that felt as if I showed favoritism towards him because I didn't follow the crowd and agree to fire him automatically. When they learned the truth about his reasons for trying to leave, they were much more understanding and realized that I was trying to be compassionate and using my own integrity to make my decisions.

I learned how important it is to keep your standards while showing compassion with your team. You have to do what is right, even when it goes against the majority. I was one of the only people that was willing to sit down with this individual and give him the opportunity to really explain his situation. I didn't let the fact that everyone else wanted to fire him affect my personal ethics. We were able to retain a valuable employee simply because I decided to give him a chance when no one else was willing to.

I think that some individuals get pressured into making decisions simply because 'everyone else' supports them. You have to remember to preserve your own integrity whenever you make decisions. If you know that something is being done that violates your ethics and the values of your company, you have to stand up and go against the crowd. You may not always receive a lot of support, but at the end of the day you'll know that you did the right thing and you might just get everyone else to realize the error in their judgement at the same time.

## Woman Maintains Integrity, Pursues New Career

I was the Managing Director at my company. I had worked there 25 years and was a manager for the last 15 years. I managed teams that varied in size from 5 people to 25 people. Around the time of the fiscal crisis, I disagreed with company policy and the approach to our core product. I was repeatedly called into meetings and I was basically told to get with the program. The program, however, was the way of covering their own mistakes in other areas. It was a struggle because I always thought of myself as a team player and my team didn't know what to do because I had to shield them from the issue. I told my employees not to do anything differently from what we've always been doing. I didn't adjust how we were doing things so it would make them feel comfortable. I had to actively encourage my people not to engage in the actions we were being asked to do because the actions were unethical.

A lot of people left because of the toxic environment. My decision to resist company policy damaged my standing in the company. They took away managing responsibilities, moved me to a smaller office, and then no office at all, but I never changed. The only thing that you have that you can control is your integrity. To me, my decision to act ethically was worth it.

This whole "ethical grey area period" was where I didn't do what they wanted me to do. Individually the decisions weren't illegal, it just didn't feel right. It was just a corporate culture that became something that I thought was a challenge. I went through a period of pushback for about five years but eventually it got to the point where I needed a new job. It's hard to get out of your comfort zone when it's how you've defined your life in a particular way. I had to redefine my life because of something I didn't believe in ethically.

I held more frequent meetings with my team to encourage them to follow our standard guidelines and I protected them. It wasn't right for them to feel any pressure, so I was the filter. I encouraged them to maintain a positive attitude and to act consistently.

One thing I didn't do is I didn't denigrate the company's actions to anybody but my family. I quietly have told my close friends. I was asked to do something that I didn't agree with and I knew it was a way to compensate for other mistakes the company had made. I pushed back and it impacted my career. It felt too much like it tested my integrity.

It turned out that I changed my feelings both about the work I did and the company I work for and I decided to leave my job. Many of the people who worked for me have left the company. I am still close with the people who worked with me at the time because we went through this bad situation together.

My biggest lesson? I think the resilience of people in the workplace and that things often turn out much better than you expect. I also think the transferability of those experiences that people have to new ethical dilemmas. The first time you encounter a situation like this, it feels so devastating. After this situation, I felt more capable and it became a barometer for how I acted.

What I would do differently? For me, I saw a great deal of passive aggression. If I had pushed back more about why I thought it was wrong, I think I would have helped resolve it for myself. Instead, I became more resentful. I was never very passive aggressive but I think I have become less so after this incident, and that it's better to confront the issue head on. It did burn bridges with people I confronted. The company overturned a lot of management so a lot of the people are new but I won't even go by the building when I'm in the area. I suppose you could say I burned the bridge behind me.

One more piece of advice? By maintaining my integrity, I protected the people around me and did not draw them into the issue. They took away my management responsibilities because I was protecting them from decisions I had made in disagreement with the company. In the absence of other criteria, you need to follow what we say we do.

Integrity is having a road map; if you have procedures you're supposed to follow, you follow them. Integrity is something you control. People go wrong when they don't do what they say they do. It's the thing that trips most people up when they get in trouble; they didn't do what they're supposed to do. Managers can make sure there's always a roadmap and that the process is well defined. People may disagree with the decision, but if you have followed the process then that's okay.

## *Regrets: Sometimes The Wrong Choice Has Even More Impact*

These everyday values based leaders admitted they were imperfect. They made regrettable decisions with others. Courageously, they reflected on the situations where the wrong choice had changed them forever. They now lead and model values based principles that allow them to respect themselves. They were grateful for second chances

**Be the Change You Wish to See In Your Company**

I faced an ethical dilemma during my first few weeks at a new company. I noticed all of my coworkers were really nice, but all seemed really defensive about the information they were providing on a certain product. It was really bizarre because as an outsider, you're just asking a few questions here and there and the mood would suddenly turn. It was palpable. I decided to investigate, and came to realize that they are telling a white lie every time someone asks them about it. They would say things like, "Well, I don't really know the answer to your question" when they knew I would not like the truthful answer. It's one thing to not broadcast things that make you look bad, but this took it a step further.

I almost left the company because of this. If it hadn't been for leaving my last job after a couple of months for an unrelated reason, I probably would have left. My choices were to either bail, stay with the company and do nothing, or do something about it. I knew I couldn't just go in and change a company. I wasn't even a manager at the time. As a new guy, I would have been fired if I called them out right away. So really I waited and tried to learn as much as I could about the business and why they behaved this way.

Once I got a leadership role and knew a little bit more, I starting shifting procedures to meet a higher ethical standard. It didn't make the company more money, but they are still operating and making plenty of money. Why lie and risk getting caught in a lie with margins and financial health like that.

It's bad business to chase a few extra bucks while risking big money down the road. The other really funny part about fixing this lie is that employee retention went up. I don't work there anymore, but so many of the people that came in after the change are still there. I am very proud of this. People would rather not lie on a daily basis, who would have thought?

Lessons learned? Carefully vet the company you are going to work for. Make sure the company aligns with your core values before jumping into a role. We are not in a recession anymore. You can afford to be a least a little picky.

## $100K in Missing Drugs Leads to Investigation

I had employee theft take place at my veterinary practice. By the time the manager became aware of the situation, the employees in question had stolen $100,000 (wholesale) in heartworm and flea treatment medications. The question on everyone's minds was, "How could this be going on right under our noses?"

Here is how. At the end of the day, Joaquin (a pseudonym for an employee) would pretend to empty the trash of the receptionist area where the medication was located on shelves to sell to clients. The accomplice named Tonya (another pseudonym) was a receptionist who had access to the products. She would give him the medicine, and he would pretend to take the trash to the dumpster but instead put the medicine in his car. Then they would meet at the gas station nearby so Joaquin could give Tonya the medicine, which she would sell on craigslist.com. After a year, the manager realized the inventory on the shelves and in the stock room did not match the quantities in the log. That is how we finally realized all this medicine was missing from the clinic.

This is a significant breach of ethics and moral fiber as employee theft over $200 is a felony and this was a large quantity of drugs that had been stolen for a long period of time. We realized that the same drugs were being sold on craigslist.com. In fact, a client had informed us when he realized he could buy the medications on craigslist.com at the wholesale value. I called the number provided and to my total surprise, Tonya answered the phone call.

My business partner and I decided to hire a private investigator to verify that Tonya was stealing and selling the drugs. To do this, the Private Investigator had to catch her in the act. He set up cameras inside the hospital and bought the meds from Tonya in a sting operation. After the investigator had caught her red-handed, he interviewed Tonya. She was the one who informed the investigator that Joaquin was helping her steal the drugs and they were sharing the profits from their craigslist sales. The investigator interviewed Joaquin and he confessed to the crimes.

My business partner and I had two options. We could either fire the employees or fire and prosecute the employees. This was a hard choice as Joaquin was pre-vet and this would ruin his chance of getting into vet school. Although this was dishonest on Joaquin's part, they felt bad for him as he had a great financial need and they felt that he did not play as big of a role as Tonya in the theft. However, Tonya had a record of theft and being a dishonest employee. Unfortunately, the manager was unaware of her previous criminal record during her employ at their veterinary practice.

We decided to fire and prosecute both employees. A deal was made within the court system and their crimes were reduced from felony to misdemeanor and they were both ordered to repay $18,000 each within an 18-month time frame. Joaquin fulfilled his sentence by repaying his debt within the given time. Tonya never has repaid any money to the employers and has no plan to do so at this time. Tonya should be in jail but unfortunately she is not, based on various legal maneuvering.

Joaquin will not be able to go to vet school and he has brought shame to himself and his family. I was very upset over this whole ordeal. It made me question people and their motives. I am no longer as trusting of others as I was prior to this theft. Also, my business partner and I lost a lot of money due to this event. Not only did we lose the money from the stolen medications, but also the cost of the private investigator and court/lawyer fees. This hurt our business.

There were many lessons that my partner and I learned from this story. First, we implemented a better system for inventory tracking and control. Second, we started running background checks on employees prior to hiring them. Lastly, we have added cameras and tightened security measures on drugs and cash by adding cabinets with lock and key.

In my opinion, honesty is always the best policy. One should try to fix things when they are small before the situation gets out of hand. People will always make mistakes and then they think they have to cover them up. Instead, it is better to be honest, come forward, and try to make things right while you still can.

We felt that Joaquin really got coerced into this situation by Tonya and the attractiveness of having much needed cash, but because he did not come forward, his life is now ruined. He can no longer go to vet school and he will always have these charges following him throughout his life.

## 95% Chance of Yes Still Means 5% Chance of No

I once had to deal with an employee who gave a preemptive go-ahead on a client's marketing content. The employee expected them to say yes and move forward rather than waiting any longer for a go ahead. The client did not approve once they responded two days later. So you can imagine what happened when a response about this product was sent to my boss, then down to me.

Thankfully the company was not going to sever the relationship, but it did make us look bad assuming that all was okay before they asked for a change. There was the suggestion of terminating the employee, but the damage wasn't high enough to warrant that option. We also could have continued a pattern of lying to the client.

After the incident, I made my employee earn my trust back. We had a talk, and I had a greater understanding of why she claimed it was okay, with concern of meeting a deadline and not wanting to delay their response any longer. However, lack of feedback did not count as a yes, and I had to make that point clear. We also emphasized to the client that they needed to respond more timely so they could meet their goals.

Our employee made sure to keep me copied on further communication with the clients, and escalated any issues. She became aware that pride was not an issue if they did not respond promptly, but the client was, in turn, responsive as well on their progress. Ironically, they did not ask for changes to marketing copy during the approval phase the next few times it happened.

You can't always trust a company to always sign off on something. If you assume that everything is okay when it really is not, and you skirt protocol in the process, that is the one time when you'll be caught in a pickle.

People will always appreciate someone who acts on their values, but especially when he or she doesn't actually wear them explicitly. It demonstrates the difference between talking and walking.

## Guns, Gossip & Girls

I had the opportunity to work with an exceptional leader that served as my role model and mentor early in my career. As this individual began to move up within the company, his brother came in to run the corporate owned business. I quickly discovered that working for his brother would be extremely different. Shortly after taking over, he began sleeping with employees and showed no interest in learning how the business operated. Not only were his actions unbecoming of a business leader, he was hurting the organization as a whole. As the situation began to worsen, I was contacted by the corporate office to answer questions about the new business owner. Although I felt loyal to his brother, I could not lie to the corporate representative and let the reputation of the company continue to suffer.

My first response to the situation was to address my concerns with the business owner. He received the feedback like I expected and refused to adjust his behavior. I was already in the process of stepping away from the situation as I was leaving for college. Shortly after starting classes, I received a phone call from the corporate office asking about the current situation of the business. Although I did not agree with how the business was being operated, I was still loyal to his brother that had taught me so much earlier in my career, and felt like I was betraying his trust if I told the truth.

Ultimately, I decided that the company's reputation was being tarnished and I had a responsibility to be truthful. After speaking with the corporate representative, I immediately called the first business owner and shared what I had observed. The current business owner was let go, based on the information I provided, along with other discoveries.

I feared that the first business owner would be upset about the situation, as it was his brother being terminated. Surprisingly, he shared that he would have done the same thing had he known. I also feel that I was given the opportunity to grow within the company as a result of being honest.

There are two main lessons I learned from this situation. The first was that your head and heart may not always agree. My heart loved this family and did not want to betray their trust. However, my head knew that what was going on was not acceptable and had to be stopped. I also realized that those who have high moral standards would never be upset with you for doing the right thing, even if it affects them in a personal way.

## Always Take The High Road

I worked for an insurance company in customer service, where I sent invoices for payments for insurance policies. I kept getting requests from customers who said they had paid, but they did not receive proof of payment. The agency owner was responsible for processing payments, so I asked him if he knew what was happening with these payments. After talking to a few people in the office, I learned that they were cashing the checks but not submitting it to the insurance companies to put policies in force. I asked my boss why checks showed up in the customer's account but we didn't have record of it. He told me the checks were probably on their way and not to worry too much about it. It was significant because I had just started working there so I didn't feel comfortable speaking up about this after talking to my boss. I felt like I should say something but didn't know who to tell or what to say.

Customers were still calling about this issue. I could lie to them and say that it was taking time to get to the insurance company, knowing that this was not the case. I could have spoken up, although I was worried my co-workers wouldn't trust me at work. It was often easier to just stay quiet and avoid the topic with customers.

I decided not to say anything, but I knew I couldn't lie to the customers so I really just acted oblivious to the situation. I would tell them I did not know but I would not use the same lies that my boss had told me. If customers asked for more information, I would forward them to my boss because I knew he was ok with telling them this lie. This isn't something I am proud of when I think back to it.

The company continued to take the checks and give the customers reasons for why their checks were not being processed. I left the company a few months after I learned that this was happening. I have not kept track of the company but I assume that they are still doing this.

The most significant thing I learned is that even if you feel like you are not compromising your values, it still affects you. I feel bad when I think about how easy it would have been to report this to someone while I was working there but I decided to take what I thought was the easy route.

Always try to do the right thing. Just because it isn't wrong, doesn't mean that it is right. I thought that if I could do my job and not ruffle any feathers, I would be doing the right thing for me and my career, but I wasn't honest and the feeling from that was worse.

## Resigned Due To Inability To Convince The Masses

During a negotiation between Management and a Union of 500 workers, two of the union members were more concerned about their personal retirement benefits instead of the benefits for the members of the Union as a whole. In this case the Company wanted to implement something called an Alternate Work Schedule that would benefit the Company and the Union. During the negotiation, the Union leadership on the negotiating committee agreed to truly endorse the contract and the change but the Union president found out that two members of the Union who were more concerned about their retirement benefits were not happy with the new proposal and were threatening to go on strike.

After the Union president's endorsement speech at the member meeting where the voting was going to take place, the two vocal members with greater self- interests delivered their message of unhappiness and unwillingness to vote for the Alternate Work Schedule. The two members were so focused on an increase of retirement benefits due to their approaching retirement that they sabotaged the entire agreement.

Out of the 506 Union members, 255 voted against and 251 voted for the proposal due to the influence of the two vocal members. The two members convinced the workers not to vote for the proposal based on the perception that the Alternate Work Schedule was not for their benefit. Workers were not aware of the real reason, the self- driven interests.

The Union President resigned and management was never able to trust the Union committee again.

The Union President resigned when he realized that his speech was not as accurate as it could have been and that much of the tension was because things were not explained in details to the Union members at the meeting. He was disappointed that he could not convince and influence his members to trust him versus the loud, vocal members. He was disappointed that he did not clarify the true motivations for the membership to hear so they could make their decision with the full set of information.

The significant thing that I learned as a result of this was the importance of good communications and influence. It is important to communicate effectively, and to think about the ultimate audience and how they will receive the message. In this case, it was also important to not under estimate that some will go to any length for their personal interests. The best scenario was not implemented because the best message was not received.

**Data Matters**

Working in a product management environment, my boss asked me to provide financial information in a way that would support the decision he wanted the board to make. I realized he was manipulating and framing the information to influence the board. I could either present the numbers honestly, without any embellishment of the information to sway the Board, or to present the numbers the way they were presented.

I ended up presenting the numbers to the Board as my supervisor initially requested. Thankfully, the Board requested additional information which made it clear that the decision he wanted them to make was not the best for the company. It set a precedent for more detailed information to be presented to the Board. It was quite clear that the Board was well informed and they wanted to make sure that all sides were evaluated.

Listen to your inner voice. Always do what is right, and when in doubt, ask.

## Stealing Hurts Everyone Involved

When I was a kid in high school I was confronted with a situation of confronting my friend. ] I saw and knew my manager was stealing from the cash register. I had really three options. Say nothing, confront the manager, or tell the district manager. I ended up confronting my manager about it. I explained that I knew and saw her steal the money from the register a couple of nights recently, and I was prepared to let others know if she didn't stop.

I lost that part-time job not long after. However, I did tell the district manager. In hindsight, I should have told her and the district manager at the same time. I think because I was being fired it looked like I was just an embittered ex-employee. I never knew what happened to my old manager. I feel I did the right thing by saying something. I know that I am true to myself and ANY company I work for, because I do not allow lying, cheating or stealing.

Truthfulness, honesty and personal responsibility will ultimately make your life so much easier. You don't have to worry about covering things up or lying to cover for previous lies. Just be yourself.

## College Creates Unneeded Course Requirements for Long Time Employees

I taught a chemistry lab at the local community college. A fellow chemistry instructor I admired called to get my opinion on a dilemma she faced. She had a student in a class who was a community college employee and only a few years away from retirement. The community college had recently implemented a policy requiring all employees of the school to take and pass certain courses in order to retain their jobs. This particular student was not going to pass a required chemistry course. The new community college requirement seemed arbitrary and unnecessary in this particular situation. My friend wanted my opinion on whether to pass or fail this student.

My friend passed the student/employee. She and I have never discussed it again. I have thought about it often. I have failed students over the 25 years I've taught, but these were younger students which did not fall under this special requirement, and I'm sure this did not negatively impact their lives. Additionally, this course would not have been beneficial for this employee.

Sometimes choices are really tough. Sometimes you have to make decisions that seem to violate your principles, but you also have to sleep at night. In making decisions, be ready to accept all consequences.

## If You Lose Character, You Can Never Get It Back

During the days of the first Internet boom, one of my former employers was involved in the business of laying out fiber optic cables to serve the internet. The company's senior vice president became interested in building cement sheds to go at the base of the cell tower. The shed would carry fat cables that would fire up DC Power equipment in batteries – enabling cell signaling. Higher management asked for a business plan since building the infrastructure for cement shelters required significant investment. Moreover, the shelter building was out of the current business model and management seemed skeptical on the project's ROI. This was my first job as a product manager, and I was part of the team to run the analysis.

After conducting the market research, the team concluded that the market was saturated with competition. The net present value was negative, which indicated this would be an unprofitable venture for the company. After presenting our analysis to the Senior VP, he essentially asked us to falsify the results and justify the viability of the project.

I could either falsify the results as directed by the Senior VP, voice my opinion to the upper management, or dismiss myself from the team. I chose the latter. After the

Senior VP knew about my dismissal from the team, he tried to play nice and convince me to rejoin the team. After I resisted that option, he became very agitated and pointed and personally threatened me. He hissed, "If you tell anyone about this, I will make sure you are fired. I will make sure your career is over". He definitely saw me as a threat to his plans.

I moved to a role of a sales manager within the same company and made a point to distance myself from the Senior VP. While this was happening, the rest of the team went ahead with the project. The company bought a $75 million rectifier company from the UK, then hired service and construction people to build demonstrations. Three years, later the company got out of the cell tower business – shut down the operations concerned to the DC rectifiers. Many people lost their jobs and the company lost $60 million.

In hindsight, I should have been bold enough to come forward. I could have saved people's jobs and money. However, this was a time before whistle blower laws were enacted, and I still take solace that I at least did not participate in the wrongdoing. You need to be true to your core solid values. In the business world, there will be a lot of temptations to do the wrong thing for personal gain – don't compromise your values. I stayed true to myself.

Always be honest with other people. Sometimes the most difficult part of being honest is being honest with oneself. If you look at your career decades later, you should not regret any decision that you made. Always be honest and you can never have a conflict. Try to be yourself and never try to imitate others. If you lose a job you can get another one, but if you lose character you can never earn it back.

**Respect Yourself And Live In An Honest Fashion**

I worked one summer at a local country club doing a variety of tasks and jobs for the golf course when I was in college. One of my responsibilities was servicing and maintaining the golf carts. I did this along with one other co-worker. There was a gas pump on-site that we used to refill the carts, and I came up with the idea to use the pump to also fill up my car...and sometimes my buddies' cars on the weekend or at night after things were closed up. I didn't think anyone would notice (there weren't any cameras, and we never had to do inventory on gas). I felt a little bad doing this at first, but assumed I wouldn't get caught and the country club was pretty rich so they could handle it. I obviously should not have been doing this, as it was stealing. I didn't view it as such at the time. I just saw it as a perk of the job. I also should have stopped before continuing this behavior for well over a month.

Eventually my employer became suspicious. Towards the end of the summer, I found out they had begun tracking the gas expenses after a sharp increase in deliveries. My boss brought my coworker and me together (since we were the only two people who had access to the pumps) and asked us who was responsible. My coworker had no idea this was going on as I had never told him. I decided to pretend not to know either. My boss didn't believe us and fired us both. I never ended up coming clean as my boss told us he'd report the individual responsible to the police.

I could have used the job, but more than that I felt absolutely horrible that I had gotten my coworker fired. Things ended up okay for him. He was able to reason with our boss (who I think suspected me over him anyway), and was rehired after a week or two.

When you do something immoral, you are eventually going to get caught no matter how careful you are. When you do, your actions are going to have a larger impact then you ever suspected – whether it is on your future, your family, or others around you. It's better to act honestly so you can respect yourself. Ever since that summer, I take the high road whenever I am in a situation where I could be dishonest. Respect yourself and live in an honest fashion. You'll feel better for it.

## Courage to Shine a Light

I had an employee come to me with a disturbing find when I served as a project manager in the U.S. overseeing a very large consumer product conglomerate's Enterprise Resource Planning ("ERP") system implementation in Latin America. The employee had come across some "financial irregularities" while reconciling the old payable system process for matching invoices to the new three way match system. The find was significant because the illegitimate expenses traced back to the company CEO in Latin America. Although this subsidiary of the company was in Latin America, the overall company was headquartered in the United States, making the activity illegal. The options at hand to remedy the situation were ; 1) "Bury it"; or 2) confront the local Finance Team (the CFO) directly with the find and let them handle it as they see fit.

I worked with one of the local accountants and gathered the appropriate due diligence on the transactions so they could not be disputed. I then turned the transaction data over to the next level of management to take to the client CFO. Unfortunately that never happened and the next level of management "buried it". That course of action was never discussed with me, and the outcome still bothers me to this day.

It turns out a financial crime was being committed, and someone trusted to bring the issue to light turned the other way. I learned several lessons from the incident: have the courage and conviction to confront the CFO of a company directly, you cannot always trust your "upline" will do the right thing or have the same integrity and ethics you do, and it's important that if you aren't seeing the outcome or actions you feel are right that you notify someone else until you see the right actions taking place.

This incident happened in 1993 and the CEO in question went on to serve for multiple succeeding years in his position. I vowed to use the experience as a "guide-post" as to the type of ethics never to tolerate in either a company or manager in the future. Have the courage to shine a light on what you think is not right.

## To Get A Raise, Get Drinks

My boss often had favorites. While at first this doesn't seem to be an issue, it often led to drinks after work and eventually promotions. I can't help but think that I was held back because I have children and didn't drink with my boss after work. Unfortunately, I didn't do anything. At the time I was afraid of adverse reactions if I were to bring it up.

I left the company after a few years. I left very bitter and unhappy with my position. I wish I would have spoken up, but been prepared to leave if I needed to. I feel like I would have left with a little more dignity. Always go with your gut feeling. Typically, your gut is giving you a good indication about a situation. I always tell my children to stick to their guns, so I wish I would have taken the same tip.

## Lies Build On Lies

My boss was pressuring me to register clients only for the month of December to meet end of the year growth goals. It was only three months into my tenure and there were pay increases on the line for me in addition to proving myself. I talked with my boss about how I felt this was unethical. He didn't agree, and since his performance was also on the line, he pushed me to follow his instructions.

However, I chose to work hard to meet the deadline honestly. I didn't meet that particular goal but hit all of my others. My boss trusted me a little less from that point on –ironic in that I made the honest decision and lost trust.

Lies build on lies. It isn't worth doing something against your code of ethics. Also, bad decisions like this will build on themselves. Those inflated numbers would have had to have been inflated again plus annual growth.

## Caring People Are Better Than Their Counterparts

I work in a small office. We were in one of our regular meetings regarding our social media efforts for the upcoming week. One group member (who is one of the most difficult people in the office to work with) came into this particular meeting and proceeded to belittle and slam the work we had done the previous week. He even got to the point where he raised his voice with his own supervisor and shrugged the supervisor's questions off by the end of the conversation.

I was uncomfortable in my role to do anything other than speak to the work we had done the previous week that was called into question. My department was very satisfied with the results from the work. The supervisor, however, began to doubt himself regarding social media since it was not his forte. During that meeting, the issue was not resolved, which spoke volumes about the manager's leadership and management skills.

After the meeting, my own supervisor asked me what had happened since the raised voices could be heard throughout the office. He was concerned that I was a target in the heated conversation. The other supervisor eventually walked in on the conversation and was confrontational with us. My own supervisor and I attributed this to misplaced anger after the previous conversation took place. In the moment, we worked to resolve the issue that concerned us, which was the work itself.

This, coupled with other events and difficulty working with the employee, still exist with multiple people throughout the office. Other leaders in the organization have raised questions with the manager of the day-to-day operations of the office. Nonetheless, he is still employed and difficult to work with, and there are no signs of either of these things changing. I was disappointed in the supervisor's handling of the situation and allowing his employee to be so disrespectful to his coworkers. I learned that his leadership and management skills still require some development, even though he's been in the position for several years.

As well-known and cliché as it is, I think treating others as you want to be treated is such an underrated way of interacting and working with other people. If you're honest, other people will appreciate that. Caring people are better than their counterparts. All of these things in a positive environment in which you treat other as you would want to be treated lead to a much happier, stable atmosphere.

## Don't Be Afraid to Hold Onto Your Values

I was the sales manager at an electronic company. My team sold cell phone subcomponents to other companies and factories. Once, I visited a new customer and tried to promote our products. That company's sales manager told me he was willing to do the business with us only if we gave him some money under table.

I didn't make the deal with the manager directly because I wanted to maintain my personal reputation and our company's as well. However, I introduced the manager to other middle men. I assumed these middlemen made the deal since we got a huge order from the middle man right away. I got promoted and the middle man made some money, as did the sales manager.

I personally will insist to do my job in an honest and ethical way. However, when you are in an industry with this kind of culture, you either learn a way to deal with it or leave. By the way, I quit about 2 years ago.

It's really your own choice how you want to do your job. Understanding the industry before you go in can help you avoid certain corporate cultures you know you will hate. My advice would be: nobody can force you to do things that you don't want to do. There's always a next customer or a next job.

## Lies and Diffusion of Power

After business school, my brother sought employment with a real estate investment trust. Despite the terrible market at the time, my brother leveraged his prior learning to become employed by a company I'll call Acme Realty Investments (ARI). He quickly rose through the ranks as a financial analyst. In the first quarter of one particular year ARI was involved in a major financial scandal that caused the company to completely reorganize. After posting earnings that positively surprised everyone within the company, ARI did some internal investigation to find out what had happened. They posted earnings amounting to $23 million dollars more than expected, a relatively large sum comparable to their size.

After investigating, the company determined that an accounting error had been made due to a switch between FIFO and LIFO accounting practices. Rather than addressing the public and announcing their problem, they chose to cover up the issue and go on pretending like the numbers were legitimate. After realizing their mistake, ARIs Chief Accounting Officer approached the CFO, CEO and Chairman to discuss the mistake and how to resolve it. The chairman coerced all them into maintaining the status quo and operating as per usual. The ARI executives, scared of the repercussions of challenging their powerful chairman, determined that it was ultimately not their responsibility to report on the situation. Ultimately a whistleblower reported them and ARC (and the chairman's fortune) plummeted overnight. The executives who supported his decision are now pending trial for fraud.

There were several unethical influence principles at play here. First and foremost, the chairman abused his power to coerce the other employees. He used his wealth and founding position as leverage against the executives. He effectively strong-armed his underlings by threatening their positions. As a flip side of this, his employees naturally expected some aspect of reciprocity by refusing to disclose the mistake to the public. Part of their 'deal' with the chairman was that there would be some benefit for themselves by keeping their mouths shut.

This could be the case with special treatment in the future of even a financial incentive. They also failed to ethically understand the consistency of their decision. Because they had made the mistake in an official capacity, it was difficult for them to admit it later because they sought consistency with their initial estimate.

To me the biggest lesson to be taken away from this is that if you know something you are doing is wrong, but there is a group decision to stick with it, one needs to be bold and surpass the chain of command. The accounting mistake made at ARI could have happened anywhere, but the decision to cover it up was a mistake that could easily be learned from and circumvented.

## Doctor's Beating Opens Investigation To Larger Criminal Activity

When I was a younger man, I always knew that I wanted to become a physician. However, my family was not wealthy and the school district that I was raised in was sub-par. I knew that I would have to work my butt off in school and obtain a scholarship to get into college. After a lot of hard work and support from family and friends, I achieved my dream by becoming a medical doctor specializing in primary care. Because of the environment in which I was raised and the support of those closest to me, I decided I wanted to practice medicine in underserved and low-income communities. This decision led me to the San Francisco Bay Area in the late 1970's.

I joined a medical clinic that was owned and operated by the father of one of my close friends. For the sake of this discussion, we will call him Dr. Alex. I enjoyed the time of mentorship and his counsel immensely! Unfortunately, Dr. Alex passed away less than 6 months from the time of my employment. That left a vacuum of leadership and direction for the medical clinic.

Dr. Alex's business partner attempted to fill that void. He began to "encourage me" to write prescriptions for "walk-in patients". These patients would walk into the clinic, go to the front reception desk, pick up their prescription, and then abruptly leave the building. I did not feel comfortable with this request so I simply ignored it and choose not to write these prescriptions. As time passed, Dr. Alex's business partner would periodically "encourage me" to write these prescriptions. Again, I ignored it.

One Saturday afternoon, I was leaving the medical clinic for lunch when a group of young Asian men swarmed me in the parking lot and brutally assaulted me. As they walked away (yes they walked, they didn't run) they declared, "You will get us those prescriptions!" I could run and hide or I could fight for what was right. I could simply place my signature on a small piece of paper which authorized them access to the drugs they desired, or I could fight to preserve the morals of my profession, the ideals of my life, and the safety of my community.

I contacted the police department and reported the assault. I notified them that the individuals demanded unauthorized access to prescription drugs. The events at the medical clinic were part of a much larger spree of crime in the San Francisco Bay Area. The individuals who assaulted me were members of an Asian gang that was wreaking havoc across the Bay Area. Their criminal activity included home invasions, drug dealing, small business extortion, and loan sharking within the impoverished community. The gang had coerced Dr. Alex's business partner to organize their prescription drug operations.

Ultimately, the U.S. Department of Justice's Drug Enforcement Administration shut down the medical clinic. Dr. Alex's business partner was stripped of his license to practice medicine within the State of California by the Medical Board of California. He was also sentenced to 4 to 5 years in state prison. The gang was broken up and the individuals were prosecuted based on the crimes they had committed.

I was simply following the rules and guidelines that were expected of me. I had no idea that I was even being asked to participate in criminal activity. I knew that I felt uncomfortable and therefore I choose to ignore the request but I did not expect that one of my colleagues was part of a larger group of criminals. Perhaps I was unaware because I was so young and trying to focus on my desire to help others. Whatever the case may be, I am a little embarrassed that I choose to dodge the request of my colleague instead of confronting him. I should have plainly asked him why he was requesting such actions on my part.

Focus on who you are as a person. What are your dreams? What are you doing to attain those dreams? Are you caring, loving, and respectful as you pursue your dreams? If you work hard, love deeply, and passionately strive for your goals, you will do very well in life. Many ills in life can be attributed to individuals who have no direction or plan for their lives, individuals acting selfishly and hurting others because of it, or people who have lost the desire to become a better version of themselves.

## Hidden Blessings

There was an important tax election for a corporate tax client that needed to be made by a deadline. My team, including myself, missed the deadline. There was a significant tax implication of not making the election, but there was also a risk that the client would fire the firm. During the status review of the client's tax return, I learned we missed the deadline and had to report the situation to our boss.

There really weren't any other options because the situation would have eventually been discovered. The only course of action was to notify the leaders of the department and the client. I also had to research whether there were any options that could be employed to get relief from our mistake. This involved talking with people from the firm's national office, which was really embarrassing.

The research and discussions uncovered a rarely used provision that basically says, under certain circumstances, when an advisor makes a mistake that the taxpayer should not be made to suffer. This relief required making statements that detailed the mistake that were made, which again was humiliating. We were able to successfully get the election made and the client did not suffer but I always felt that some of the leaders of the practice no longer trusted me.

I always felt that the staff member who had been responsible for working on the election had not taken enough responsibility. As a result, I think I was not able to work on more interesting and challenging projects. From a positive perspective, it did eventually interest me in changing the direction of my career, which eventually opened up other opportunities.

The most significant thing I learned that it's best to address your problem as soon as you know about them. Procrastinating just makes things worse. I also learned that it's important to trust but verify.

## Employee Whistle Blower Turns in Fraudulent Car Loan Applications

When I was 25, I worked in the car business in finance and insurance (F/I) for a local dealership. Soon after I started, everyone was switched to a mostly commission based pay scale. Sales managers who previously did F/I asked me to doctor some loan applications to make the customer's income greater than it was in order to secure the loan and sell more cars. I could have either gone along with the plan to doctor the loan applications and increase all of their sales commissions, or I could refuse. If I refused, I could have raised the issue with the owner or not said anything.

I initially refused and did not immediately raise the issue. Later, when hearing about some of the sales from that week, I realized that the Sales Manager had doctored the loan applications himself after I refused to do it for him. He had filed them as his sales and his applications, so he would get all the commission. Once I learned that, I decided to alert the owner on the situation. The owner never did anything as far as I know. I made the decision to leave the company for self-preservation. Within six months of leaving the company, the sales manager was fired, convicted of fraud, and went to prison.

There is no room for grey areas when it comes to ethics. Ethics are more than not being unethical yourself, they are preventing others from doing unethical things as well. Before committing to a questionable decision, I ask myself, “Could I sleep with this at night if I made this decision?” It has made me a better leader and has earned me the trust of my coworkers.

## Find a Career that Fits Your Morals

I worked for a small regional bank that was purchased by a much larger national bank. I served as Assistant Vice President at the headquarters building. The larger national bank that purchased our bank brought in an outside hire to a Vice President position. The new VP requested that I begin to learn more and broaden my horizons so I could advance. The VP said I could start coming to the month-end close out meetings. The month end close out meeting was a process to review the financials for the bank. I was just an observer in these meetings and I didn't feel like I could speak up.

I only went to a couple of the meetings. The meetings would mainly focus on where we looked on our bottom line compared from last month and how that varied from where did corporate want us to be. If we were not meeting corporate expectations, meeting participants would ask what they could move to next quarter to make it look better. Or how could we make the bottom line look thicker? Most importantly, they began falsifying little bits of information to match what corporate wanted them to do.

Thinking back on it now, I should have said something, but the question is who would I have told? It got to the point where I didn't want to go to work, it wasn't a good environment for me emotionally and ethically, so I eventually resigned. I had never quit a job without another job waiting, but it wasn't worth it. A paycheck isn't worth the pull on your well-being. I ended up resigning from the organization.

I wish I would have given a better reason for resigning. I should have told someone what was going on. During the exit interview, I told HR that the newly relocated headquarters (which was an hour further from where I live) was my reason for resignation. I found another job in the public sector, working for the county at half pay but I was certainly much healthier emotionally and out of that environment where they weren't doing the right thing. Deciding whether to remain or leave the small regional bank was very stressful. It really made me think about what was important to me as a person.

What's the tradeoff you're willing to take between career and what's right? Sometimes that tradeoff leads you down paths where you're not quite sure what's going to happen. I vowed from that point on that I would never work in the financial private sector because I had seen what goes on behind the scenes and it wasn't for me. It's interesting over the last few years we've seen that set of malicious behaviors come to light with the culture and the ethics at banks. Customers and employees aren't important, only the bottom line is important and we'll do whatever it takes to get there.

It was tough for a while since I was working a cashier job for half the pay I was making before. Most importantly, though was I could live with myself with this decision. To me that's more important than how much money you have in the bank.

I learned something very significant from this experience. I learned about what I wanted from my profession. I learned about being a supervisor, what to do and what not to do, and I learned a lot about myself. You have to find the right situation and a career that matches your emotional and moral standards.

I've always lived with the idea that I need to leave this Earth having contributed to making it better, in some way. I think we, as human beings, have a responsibility to contribute to the betterment of mankind. Not everybody has the talent to contribute in a huge way, but I can leave the world a better place by being tactfully honest with people and understanding where other people are coming from.

You can use differences and diversity to make a team that is bigger than the people that are in it. I think that we need to take the long view on things. This is hard to do because sometimes we let our emotions and misinterpretations get in the way. You have to deliberately overlook the slights and take the long view on things and sometimes that long view is good for you personally and sometimes it's not.

**True Test of Leadership Comes from Inside a Crucible**

Brent Landry (a pseudonym) was on his first deployment to Iraq as a commander. Once he arrived into country, the armored vehicles he was promised were not delivered. He still had a requirement to conduct security patrols in his area of responsibility, despite not having armored vehicle to protect his personnel in an area that was known to have a high incidence of improvised explosive devices. He was in a hot environment, which at times could be explosive, Brent felt that he and his team were inside a crucible.

Brent had two options at the time, to sit inside his fortified base and wait to be attacked or to go out, conduct security patrols and accomplish the mission his unit was given. He conducted his risk mitigation analysis and surveyed his team to reach a consensus to continue operations without armored vehicles. His personnel got very creative with homemade armor, wood, sandbags and scrap metal to improvise and offer some additional protection. He and his team also created protocols that no security detail would go out the gate without a reserve rapid reaction force standing by to assist if needed. His team also maxed out its communication lines by having relay patrols support teams that were on the perimeter of the area of responsibility. All of this helped mitigate the risk.

During the yearlong deployment, Brent's team was hit by numerous improvised explosive devices and his security patrols were commonly engaged by insurgents. All 173 members of Brent's team returned home alive. Brent and his leadership team worked hard to build confidence in his team. As they continued to have success in the region, they also gained the trust of the Iraqi Military and Police. This helped to further reduce the risk of attacks and created a more stable local environment.

Eventually, an executive officer toured Brent's base and recognized the lack of armored vehicles. The company was provided the required equipment shortly after the visit. With the addition of better equipment, Brent's group continued to conduct itself with the same proven tactics with great success.

Brent's goal was bringing home every single member of his team. He knew that to do that, he would have to leverage the creativity, ingenuity and hard work of every single member of his team. He also created an environment of trust, where his team knew that he was pushing for the necessary resources at every opportunity. Brent also routinely went out of the wire with his team leading from the front and he required all the leaders on his staff to do the same. Brent stated "Take care of people, they will take care of you and they will figure out how to get it done."

Lessons learned? Live the values, if your living them it is easy to talk about them and share them with others. Brent feels that a three word phrase from his father has formed his leadership style, "Just don't quit."

## Money, Values, and Politics Take Down High School Principal

My first job out of college was a teaching and coaching position at a college preparatory high school. Three years into my tenure, the principal was pressured to leave the role by members of the school's board, all of whom were non-educators. From my vantage point, the pressure stemmed from a series of "misdemeanor" offenses with budgets: the kind of which I suspected were common at most schools in the district. The incident was significant because I remembered thinking, "You can do a good job, but in settings like this, where political agendas are involved, even misdemeanors can be your undoing."

The principal could have had any number of responses. He could have lashed out, and taken an offensive approach to defending his decisions. He could have made the case that if other principals were to have been similarly investigated, the same issues would be discovered. He was in a unique dilemma which called for him to display humility to his accusers. He chose to demonstrate all the tenants of his values. He mounted a vigorous, yet humble, defense of his actions, and eventually moved to another school in another district. The new principal proved to be friendlier to the board, but inept at running the school. I think many of us teachers felt some disappointment in ourselves for not showing more support or more solidarity behind our boss.

As a young professional, I learned that not everyone – even those charged with leadership and oversight – has scruples. I was naïve to that point before. In the end, you have to be able to live with your decisions. They won't all be good ones; some will have bad outcomes. However, you have to be satisfied if you made them with good intentions and a clear conscience.

## My Last Company Was a Fraud

I realized that my company was a fraud. It was a very complicated situation that was well orchestrated amongst key principal leaders. Even as a close insider, I didn't initially suspect a problem. The company's core service offering had been brought to market over a decade ago then sold off to a private equity firm. After the buying firm made several failed attempts to cash out, such as foreign and domestic IPOs, they decided to invest more in the company mainly because the SEC required that the current product continue to be supported as a part of the initial acquisition deal.

The beginning of the problem started when the former CEO, who we'll call "Pat", was installed as a board observer and a clueless figurehead was installed as the CEO. Pat, who qualifies as an "evil genius", ensured that a fellow conspirator, "Cris" was hired as the CTO. Together Pat and Cris, shot down every business strategy my team proposed. At first, I thought they were just obtuse, then I came to realize that Pat and Cris were actively trying to devalue the company so they could buy it back at a bargain.

I felt I had four major options: working within the company to make changes, quietly leaving the company, becoming a whistleblower, or ignoring the issue. Initially, I tried to work for change within the company and received personal threats as a result. The deck was again stacked to Pat's advantage who installed a young, puppet CFO who was happy to do whatever he was told due to blind ambition. The Chief Counsel quit several months previously so the job of addressing my complaint fell to HR.

The soon to retire HR executive seemed like he sincerely wanted to help, but the figurehead CEO was too clueless to help. The complicating factor was that much of the information to corroborate my charges came from other members of my team who wanted to remain anonymous. I consulted with outside counsel and found a way to file a report with the SEC. Basically, I chose the whistleblower option. The SEC has not acted on the report yet, but I did find a path to protect those who wished to remain anonymous and helped them find new job opportunities. Also, as I was deciding to close this door, another door opened for me.

There are many lessons to be learned: Ambition often clouds people's judgment. The SEC has limited influence over M&A. With boards expected to self-monitor, there is a lot of room for malfeasance. The SEC is not set up to deal with anything more complex than a smoking-gun email that says "This is how we're cooking the books...!" The fact that this case was death by a thousand cuts makes it unlikely that the SEC will know what to do with it.

It's OK to search for an ethical path to a resolution, without having to fall on the sword. Do what you can to ensure self-preservation is not a factor in your decision process. It may not always be the easiest path, but I still firmly believe that doing the right thing works out in the end.

## Next Time You Might Not Get a Second Chance

The first job I ever had was working the cash register at a retail store. At first, I enjoyed being part of the working world: there's nothing like the feeling of depositing your first paycheck. However, I soon began to dislike the job. The hours were long, and I had to be on my feet the entire time. When I got hungry during my shift, I would usually steal a something small from my aisle: nuts, crackers, or a candy bar. I was always careful to be sure management would never catch me. This developed into a sort of habit. Nearly every shift, I would steal a small food item.

One of the ways I rationalized this was by telling myself that the retailer was a big soulless corporation. They pay employees very little, and they frequently cut employee's hours to save money. Moreover, they were ridiculously successful. Some petty theft would barely affect their bottom line.

As time went on, I became bolder with my theft. Soon I was stealing pens, batteries, and cigarette lighters. I was still keeping things safe and small, so I was able to avoid being caught. It was also around this time that I realized something else. I enjoyed stealing. The thrill made each shift a little less monotonous. One day, however, I pushed my luck a little too far.

Back in the days before music streaming, people had to pay for their music on iTunes. There were still ways to get music for free of course, but I figured if I could steal an iTunes gift card, the music would be free anyway. This theft required a bit more planning than usual. In order for an iTunes gift card to be activated, it has to be scanned by a register. When a customer came in with a huge order, I would scan the card in with their other items, but then keep it for myself. This time, I was stealing from individual people, but I didn't care. I just enjoyed the rush it gave me. I did this three times, and after some time passed, I was sure I had gotten away with it.

A few weeks later, I was quietly working at my register. It was a day like any other: until the manager called me into his office. He was sitting there with a woman I had never seen before. Immediately, I knew what it was about. I tried to play dumb for as long as I could, but it was over. The people who had the gift cards charged to their receipts had come back to complain, which tipped them off to look back through security footage. They had me on camera. At this point, the reality of the situation came crashing down on me. Stealing is wrong, especially when the victim is just an average person trying to buy groceries. I apologized profusely, and only asked the woman (who was in charge of security at several other retail stores in the area) to do what she thought was fair.

She decided to have mercy on me, only because her own son had been involved in a similar situation with much more dire consequences. I had to pay reparations and I was fired, but no charges were ever filed. No one outside of the three people in that room would know what had happened. Thankfully, I was able to find another job quickly and put the experience behind me. To this day, I have never stolen anything else. That experience scared me straight.

Always strive to live a moral life. Develop values and practice them. I was fortunate enough to receive a second chance, but not everyone else is. One mistake can ruin your life, so always be careful about breaching your code of ethics.

## County Makes Tough But Appropriate Decision For All 30,000 Residents

I once had a job as a county manager in another state. The county was average to below-average in size, but had one of the top five highest tax bases in the state. My superiors asked me to raise the sales taxes by 1.5 percent on the dollar so they could redistribute those taxes to meet Medicaid needs. The board of commissioners met with the county management team and informed me and the other managers of this decision. They instructed us not to share the information with the townships until the approval was made and the changes went into effect.

The change in sales tax rate would affect citizens and tax bases for several towns within the county. Ultimately, this would be negative news for the tax paying citizens. The townships, mayors, and other political powers were already preparing their budgets for submittal. I had only a few weeks to think about the consequences that I could face if I let the mayors (my bosses) know what was about to happen. I wasn't in a position to challenge the board on the latest decision. I reached out to several other managers across the region to get their insights on what I should do. Some managers in the region instructed me to talk with individual members of the board about letting the townships know in advance. Other managers basically told me that I should just do as they say.

I kept the decision to myself and with my management team until one month before the announcement was made. I made a phone call to the board and gave justification to why I needed to tell the mayors. The majority of the board was ok with the decision. I informed all townships, mayors, and other political parties involved. I wasn't going to lose my job over this announcement, however, I didn't have the heart to not inform these key stakeholders. Some mayors were displeased with the announcement based on timing. Other mayors didn't think timing was an issue and thought a change may happen as every sales tax and distribution is implemented by county commissioners.

The board's decision taught me the impact of redistributing revenue from one unit of government to another unit of government. It made me focus on budget policy and investment decisions made within the county. I learned how consequential decisions can be felt downstream even if they are made for the right reasons. Live your life affixed to those values; wake up every day and challenge yourself to exceed those moral values.

**Pennies or Peace?**

I was working with a non-profit organization that helps kids with special needs. There was a time when I helped them organize a fundraiser to raise money for gathering funds towards the kid's college needs. We collected and documented all the funds received. Three months after the fundraiser, a nice lady bumped into me and gave me money for the program, which was already over. The kids had already gone to college and the expenses were taken care of. I had an option to just keep the money without communicating with anyone about it. I was also just a student then and I really needed money. It was a tricky situation. I could just keep the money for my own needs as a student. The other option was to drive all the way to the NGO just to give them that amount, which I figured wasn't their biggest concern since the program was already over.

At first, I kept the money. I was just a needy student, thinking that it was probably a meager amount that the NGO wouldn't care about. The long drive did not feel worth it either. But I couldn't live with that, and after contemplating about it for two whole days; I finally decided to return the money that belonged to them.

I learned the important lesson that doing the right thing is always the best thing. I teach my kids the same. It might be difficult initially, but you will never regret it or feel ashamed about it. I learned also that never take anything that is not yours. It is what we are taught as kids, however as we grow up, sometimes it is a tough choice to make. Always stick to your values, no matter how silly or sticky the situation.

## The Means Do Not Justify the Ends

One of my managers was taking parts from the printing company we worked for and reselling them to a third party company. This was a serious ethical dilemma because he was my manager and it was difficult for me to tell him he shouldn't do that. It was significant because they were cheating the company and making unethical decisions. Unfortunately, upper management caught on and fired him. Luckily, the people who thought about doing the same, and who I convinced otherwise, were able to keep their jobs.

This sad experience solidified my moral belief that you should always be honest. Just because you see money lying around doesn't mean you should be able to take it. People are always watching. It's our responsibility to behave as honest employees. There is no such thing as easy money. You need to work hard and honest to achieve good things in your life. At the end of the day, what really matters is how you feel when you get home.

Lesson Learned? Money is not everything. It is what you do at work, the work ethics and hard work is what is important.

### *Relationships: Personal Relationships May Make For The Toughest Choices*

As you read these stories, you will realize the heart-wrenching stress our values based leaders endured as they confronted family, friends, mentors, clients, co-workers, and managers. Their personal relationships could have negatively influenced our leaders to ignore the inappropriate behaviors, but they pursued the ethical approach. The choices made were not about popular or easy choices, but they were the right choice.

These stories reflect the topic of trust as well. "If you can't be trusted, you cannot be a leader".

## Respect From An Afghan Warlord

Background: December, 2001. Post 9/11, I was part of a senior military office that was sent to Afghanistan to represent the United States to the Northern Warlords. This was of vital importance in the early stages of the war. We needed their support in the Northern Afghanistan to form a coalition to work within the country. After countless meeting and negotiations on several issues, I encountered a challenging situation.

I was meeting one of the major tribal leaders (warlord) in Afghanistan. We were discussing releasing a prisoner to United States custody. This prisoner was perceived to be of value. Numerous attempts to gain custody of him had already failed prior to this meeting. The tribal leader stated that he would release the individual to me if I would simply declare that I was an officer of the United Nations and not a United States Military senior officer.

There were only two options in resolving this situation. I could misrepresent myself as a United Nations officer and appease his concerns for being seen a puppet to the US. Alternately, I could state I was a professional officer and a senior representative of the United States Government and that I could not disgrace myself, my profession, or the United States by openly admitting to a lie.

I took the second option, explaining to the tribal leader that like him, I was a soldier who had fought with my soldiers. As a professional senior officer, I could not disgrace my Country, my military, or myself by admitting to a lie publicly just to ascertain this prisoner. I told him it was important for us both to understand the importance of cooperation and respect.

The tribal leader stood and moved toward me. I stood to meet him. He extended his hand and stated that he understood my position completely. He stated as a senior military leader himself (the senior leader in his tribe) he was in total agreement with me. He further stated that we were to come to his residence that evening to take custody of the said prisoner.

Others that were present and had been involved in trying to gain custody of this individual on many other occasions were somewhat astonished by the dramatic change in the tribal leader's attitude and his sudden willingness to release the individual to me.

Stay true to your beliefs, ethics, and being honest with those you interact with is absolutely the best option to take in all situations. People will respect a person who stands by their convictions.

## Show Me the Money

We must make choices between right and wrong all the time in our personal and professional worlds. I have had situations throughout my career in which the right path was not always the easiest one. I am in charge of University Relations at my company and tend to forge strong relationships with interns. Some interns are stronger than others. I developed a close mentorship with one particular intern who was motivated, passionate, and hardworking. He was on his way to a full time offer. However, the company wanted him to go across the country to our other site. He confided in me that he wished to stay local and I assisted in making that happen.

The intern received a local full time offer. He asked me if I would look it over and give him details regarding the salary. He wanted information regarding the highest salary he could potentially get, which is highly confidential information. I had many paths I could have taken in this scenario. I could have given him the information, given him information about other offers, or taught him how to negotiate his offer with his hiring manager. I ultimately chose the ethical route of helping him navigate his negotiation.

I began by listening to what he was looking for, and told him to consider his interests when contemplating any full time offer. I told him to think about the following question: "Do you believe in what the company believes in?" This is crucial in determining the appropriate culture fit with an organization. Additionally, I told him to factor in potential opportunities for growth within every company into his decision as well. I ultimately did not give him the information, but chose to coach him on negotiating, which is a lifelong professional skill he can use. I taught him that work is more than money.

He was disappointed in my decision, but he understood. My relationship with him was not tarnished and I didn't think badly of him for asking. In the end, I stayed true to my core beliefs and he got some great advice. He ended up accepting an offer from a different company because they offered to pay for his Master's degree while he worked.

The most significant thing that I learned from this sticky situation is to stick to your beliefs. Had I told him the maximum salary he could get, he would have had a leg up on the other applicants. I didn't want to give him differential treatment just because I admired him and thought he was an outstanding individual. I also wanted to teach him a lesson. I don't think he would have been able to have that conversation with any other business professional. He pushed the envelope by asking me that question.

It was a good lesson for me in that I realized I don't have to cave to every request that comes to me. There are rules and policies in place for a reason. Who knows what could have happened had I given him that information? He could have shared that confidential information with others.

I stuck to my core values, while teaching him an important lesson in the process. Ultimately, as a business professional, you have to think about how your decisions will impact the company and not just yourself.

## Adhering To Your Personal Code Of Conduct

I was a manager at a company going through an acquisition. As part of this process, I was required to provide an itemized list confirming all of my hourly employees' timesheets were correct and my full time employees' PTO balances were up to date. This was important and required accuracy because it had a direct impact on the value of our company for the sale. It also impacted the employees' post-acquisition deal (either a job offer with the acquiring company or a severance package).

I had an employee whose timesheets and balances were not all accounted for and were significantly off when comparing actual time out of office vs our HR system. Taking no action would give the employee close to $1000 more in her offer. I could have let this slide, as there was no way outside of my word from knowing if her balances were accurate. The individual was also a personal friend outside of work which added a different type of pressure to the situation. Complicating this situation was that I was not personally excited about the acquisition, so it would have felt good to stick it to the company a bit.

I could have done nothing and let the employee know I was 'doing her a favor'. I also had the option to do the right thing and adjust her balances fully. Ultimately, I made sure her balances were reflected accurately. I had a direct conversation with her, she was not happy about it and pressured me to make a different decision, but I did not back down.

Things turned out well in the end. She was able to understand that this was a professional decision, so it didn't impact our personal relationship. It did lead her to have a lower package then she originally planned, which had a small financial ramification for her. She actually ended up taking responsibility for this at the end, since she should have been keeping her time up to date in our system. From my end, I think it looked good to my superiors that I actually made changes in my employees' records as this showed I was taking things seriously.

You need to have your own code of ethics and stick with it. You'll make the right decision as long as you live by your code and are firm and honest with your actions (at least most of the time).

## It's Not Enough To Come Up With A Problem, Come Up With A Solution

A few years ago, I was helping on a product launch. For any kind of launch, you have to work with multiple departments like sales, local marketing, order entry, and global marketing. This launch was significant because it was one of our company's main growth drivers for the next year. After speaking with one person in order entry, I figured out that local marketing would not be ready for the launch on time, but none of the supervisors knew. The launch being late could have a significant effect on growth the next year.

I could either tell one of the managers, keep my mouth shut, or speak with the person in local marketing that was in charge of the product launch. Either way, I knew we needed a plan to make up for the lack of growth due to the late product launch. I decided to meet with the person in local marketing that was in charge of the product launch. I didn't want to push any buttons in the team since I was fairly new at the time.

I explained how it was important to tell the managers. Although being only two months late may not seem like a big deal to him, there could be numerous repercussions for the company as a whole since everyone counted on it as one of main growth drivers. The local marketing representative ended up understanding and talking to his manager.

It's better to explain a situation in case someone doesn't understand the effect of what they're doing than to simply stay quiet or tell on them. That way, we can figure out a solution instead of calling out a problem. It's not enough to come up with a problem, you need to come up with a solution instead.

## You Cannot Compromise Integrity, Even With Friends

In the military, I was the company commander of a troop of 40. As commander, I not only lead my team, but became personally close to my troops under me. One individual who reported to me became a buddy of mine. In this situation, I needed to make sure that my entire troop could pass the required physical test. My buddy was having difficulty preparing for the physical test. To help him pass his physical test, I spent more time prepping him so that he would pass the test. After he passed his test, I learned that he cheated in order to pass the physical. I was confronted with the situation of confronting my friend. Knowing that by turning him in, I would put both a financial burden on him and put a strain on our relationship.

At the end of the day, I had to report my direct report, my friend. It was necessary because I needed to do what was right for my team. There were some of my team that didn't pass, and I needed to be fair. I also considered the high importance of integrity. In the military, not being honest can be costly – your team's lives are at stake.

I pulled my friend to the side and had a one-on-one conversation, as a friend. I had the conversation where I told him that I was aware of his cheating, and was going to reprimand him. I wanted to let him know that it was nothing personal, and that I needed to fulfil my duties based on my position as commander and leader. After having the friend to friend discussion, I then brought him into the formal military process of reprimanding him for his actions.

My friend was sent back a month, lost pay, and the actions were formally written in his file. He also went through a reprimanding process for the military called captain's mast. It impacted our relationship initially. My friend took it very personally, considering me as a whistleblower that was no longer trustworthy. Over time, we began to rebuild our relationship and he realized that the situation really was not personal. He needed to take responsibility for his actions, and I needed to do my due diligence and enforce the policy in my position as commander of the troop.

I learned I needed to do a 'gut check' in order to do the right thing. You cannot compromise integrity over friendship. It was very important to me to do the right thing, and maintain leadership position within my team. I also learned that people would have said what they would have done, but you never know until you are in that situation. It's easier to talk the talk, than walk the walk.

## Honesty Saves Event

I was in charge of supervising a corporate multiday event that linked to a major corporate initiative. I had to ensure everything was completed on schedule, that everyone in the team was participating, keeping an eye on the budget (since my company was the financier of the operation), and bringing in creative ideas. Although there was a lot of interest in the positions on the team, eventually no one wanted to lead the team except for one person. Naturally, the person became the team leader. Very soon, I began to notice the team leader was not performing as well as he should: meetings were unorganized, work he should do was not done at the agreed upon time, and other team members started to become unmotivated due to the lack of participation of the team leader.

There were multiple options. One option was to provide him with feedback and help him to improve his leadership. The second option was to depose the current team leader and elect a new one. The third option was to continue as it was going and hope for the best. Since I was carrying final responsibility for both financial health of the event and project success, I had to intervene. I sat down with the team leader to share my perception on his performance with him. I had to be honest about his missteps and tried to help him in the process of development. I tried to teach him how to organize meetings and to make him aware of the fact that his efforts were an example for the rest. I emphasized that if he did nothing, the rest of the team would do nothing.

The team leader was very glad that I told him the truth and he gladly accepted my help. It helped to improve the meetings and motivated the rest of the team to work within the schedule. The team now had a better and motivating team leader to lead them to a successful event!

People are not always offended by critics. Many people embrace comments, because that makes them improve themselves. If no one ever told them, they could never improve that part of themselves. This is also what I experienced in other work situations and what I find most useful myself.

## Personal Friendships Can Be Misused In The Business World

As Human Resource Manager, I was approached by a non-exempt employee from the Finance Department. She wanted to tell me about a recent incident she experienced and wanted my advice on how she should best handle it.

She told me that a manager in the Operations Department had asked her out to lunch at a restaurant to discuss an upcoming opening in his department reporting to him. He said that he was very impressed with her and was prepared to offer her the position if she were interested. This was an exempt position and would represent a two-grade promotion and increased salary. He said that he could not tell her the exact amount of the increase because that would be calculated be Human Resources, but it would be "significant".

When she asked about when the opening would be "posted" on our job posting system, he told her he would try to arrange for this particular opening not to be posted. This employee felt uncomfortable about this and asked her best friend (my secretary) what she should do. My secretary told her she should discuss all of this with me, which she did.

A complicating factor was that this Operations Manager was a very good personal friend of mine. We ate lunch together, bowled together, and played softball together. Further, he had confided in me on numerous occasions how attractive he had found this employee.

I could have dealt with this a few ways. I could have met with this Operations Manager and try keep the incident low key. I tried to explain how he put himself, and me, in a difficult position by compromising the integrity of the job posting system. He said that since we were good friends, I could keep this quiet and we could "work something out." Alternatively, I could go to the VP of Finance and report the problem.

I went to the VP of Finance and gave him the details how one of his employees was approached and offered a promotional opportunity by this manager, circumventing the company's policy on job postings. The VP of Finance met with him, reprimanded him, but did not think he should be terminated. Ultimately this ended the issue because this newly created open position was determined to be unnecessary and was removed from the budgeted headcount.

The most significant result was that I felt much better about the outcome but was disappointed in the fact that a good friend would use our friendship to compromise my values. I learned that it's easier said than done to report your friend if they violated ethics. I'm happy I trusted my instincts, though. Once you act against your values, and your co-workers or family see that, it can be difficult for you to earn their trust back. Stay true to who you are.

## There are No Exceptions to the Rules

When I was managing a company, two of my top performing employees falsified hours that they worked during a holiday. We never had this issue before. Even though both of them performed excellent work, their values were now questionable because they were trying to steal from the company. My options were to either terminate the employees or simply issue a written warning.

Further investigation was required to determine if this was a one-time event or a recurring incident. Clock-in and clock-out time reports were compared with hours of work reported. For one employee, falsifying hours worked had been a repeat offense so this employee was terminated. For the other employee, this was a one-time offense and was given a written warning. Morale was low for the other employees especially since we were short-staffed already.

The most important thing I learned was that, sometimes, high performing employees don't always have values aligned with the company.

## Doing the Right Thing Brings the Right Result

I was responsible for solving a business issue regarding a previously negotiated fixed price contract with one of our key customers. The relationship between my company and our customer had become tenuous, because they accused us of not living up to our end of the contract. In reviewing the contract terms, I did not agree with the accusation, and I felt that we were honoring the terms as stated. As such, I created a plan for negotiating the terms in order to improve the relationship.

This customer was very significant to our business. Not only was our current contract worth a lot of money, but winning future business from this customer could have been impacted by the outcome of this situation. My manager became involved in the negotiations.

From the start, I questioned his involvement as he was a former employee of this customer, and had negotiated this contract with my company at the time he was working for them. From my view, this was a conflict of interest, and I questioned his motivation for involvement. He should have recused himself. Nevertheless, he became involved in the negotiations, and I felt that he was negotiating against me. I would meet with the customer to work on specific terms of the agreement, but later I would find out that my boss had separate conversations with senior members of the customer.

These conversations involved negotiation terms that undercut the ones I had discussed. He was weakening our position with this customer. I felt that my boss's interests were not best aligned with his current employer (my company), but rather his former employer. He was trying to preserve his relationship with them and his legacy.

I felt that I had three options. In following the chain of command, he was my boss and I could leave the situation alone and let him continue to be involved. My second option was to approach him directly about the situation, and to ask him to step out of the negotiations. My third option was to go over his head and inform our COO of my concerns.

I decided to first approach my boss directly. I told him that I felt his involvement was a conflict of interest. I suggested that all negotiations with the customer go through me. I told him that his continued involvement was jeopardizing our positioning and our long-term relationship with this key account. He did not take this advice well, so I went directly to our COO. I told him that my boss was putting our company in a difficult situation with our customer, and I suggested that he ask my boss to pull out of the conversations regarding the contract with our customer.

The COO supported me and asked my boss to step out of the conversations and to let me be the point person for all negotiation discussions. My boss ultimately also made the decision to pull out. I was able to renegotiate the contracted terms and put our company back into a good position with the customer. This has created a long lasting positive relationship between my company and this key customer for many years.

This ordeal also had a positive impact on our relationship with the customer. Both companies emerged with mutual respect for each other. This has led to a strong, mutually beneficial relationship built on trust and appropriate accountability.

The most significant thing I learned is that you have to assume that people are going into situations for the right reasons and with the right intentions. Sometimes those reasons are not clear and can get clouded by other motivations that can compromise their judgment. I also believe that you have to "stick to your guns" when you think that something isn't right. Don't waiver or question your judgment and take action accordingly.

## Doing What Is Right – Not Just What Is Ordered

I faced an ethical dilemma while performing my duties as associate superintendent in the county school system. Part of my duties were to fill staff openings in the several school systems, including principals. I was also charged with executing discipline (including termination) of principals and other high level employees when needed. My boss, the head superintendent of county schools, did not always agree with my managerial style or my choice in personnel. The ethical dilemma occurred when he demanded a certain employee be fired or hired, depending on the circumstance, without giving me a proper reason.

He might say that he didn't like that particular employee, or had another person in mind that he would rather have the job. The employee's job performance was not the number one reason for dismissal. My boss often interjected his preference and his favored candidate for new principal hires often because he had the advantage of a personal connection. In most cases where my boss stated his opinion, he also put pressure on me to sway my decision. These episodes led to stress and tension, and I had to decide which candidate to choose.

Once, I was tasked with choosing a principal among three equally strong candidates. Two candidates were local to the community, and were favored by most because of this fact. The lone candidate from outside had no inside backing, and I was pressured to eliminate him from consideration. I used my own judgment and gut feelings and chose the outside candidate, because I felt right about him. The chosen candidate became an outstanding principal. The other two candidates eventually became principals as well, but I feel like I made the correct decision and chose the strongest candidate (despite the outside pressure).

## Urgency Required to Save Underage Rape Victim

A distant cousin, who is now in the healthcare industry, was a medical school aspirant at some point, and was job-shadowing a doctor at a hospital in India. She saw a 13-year old rape victim brought into emergency care. The little girl had undergone multiple internal injuries, and was in a state of severe trauma. Her family didn't know what to do. Instead of providing care to the patient, the doctor got entangled with police matters. Even the nurses didn't want to see the patient until the doctor stepped in.

The little girl's family was desperately yearning for help. My cousin really wanted to help her, but she knew she wasn't allowed to do so. The patient's 17-year old sister came up to my cousin and asked her if she could do anything to ease her sister's pain. My cousin felt like it was a test for her. Should she do something or should she simply watch because she was just an intern? She stood up and walked towards the doctor who was still tied up with the police officer.

With crossed arms, she stood in front of them. Her firm resolute tone carried a sense of frustration that stemmed from the stagnant status-quo. She asked them, "What are you guys doing?" It probably wasn't her place to remind the doctor of his priorities, but she had to do something. The doctor realized what needed to be done and took action. Quickly switching gears, she lowered her voice to talk to the patient's family and reassured them of the care that their child was going to receive. The patient's sister came up to my cousin later to thank her.

My cousin had no formal authority over the doctor to influence his actions. However, she reasoned with the doctor about what they should be doing, which is treating the patient at this time rather than getting involved in police matters. If she had to do it again, she would've done the same thing, just a little bit sooner so that the patient didn't have to wait and suffer for the long time she had to. Sometimes doing what is right trumps workplace status. Always put your integrity first.

## Don't Date the Bartender

At a past job, I worked with a team of other young and relatively inexperienced "managers" similar to myself. We were leading a startup, and were responsible for the marketing and operations of several restaurants, including the staff that worked there. One of my fellow managers was dating a staff member, which was discouraged, but had not been formally outlawed in our young company. I knew about this, and I knew that the manager was giving certain benefits and advantages to the staff member. The manager's actions caused other staff members to feel resentful. Ultimately, I was not a superior to this manager, but I was aware that if our CEO found out about their relationship, it could spell a major problem for my friend and colleague.

In terms of influence, I had an interesting gauntlet to navigate. I wanted my friend and colleague to stop the behavior which I thought was unethical (giving perks to an employee as a result of a romantic relationship), and I wanted to do so for both professional and personal reasons. I did not have gross moral objections to the entire situation, but I knew it was really going to cause bigger problems if it wasn't addressed. My decision to not date a staff member, and therefore "leading by example" was not a good or direct enough alternative.

I knew that I could easily take this issue up the chain and let the CEO deal with the situation, but doing that felt to too harsh. I was worried that it would get my friend fired. My ethical dilemma was: did I have a responsibility to report this up the chain? Should I give my friend and colleague a chance to recognize what was happening and make it right?

In the end, I approached my friend and colleague about the situation in a somewhat unique way. As we sat to lunch, I asked him several "rhetorical" questions about a "similar situation" and how he would feel about it if he were in my position. He quickly understood through the line of questioning that I was more or less telling him about the dilemma I was facing. He understood I wanted him to help me out of the situation by changing or eliminating the problematic behavior. In this situation, the tactic worked well. He immediately ended the relationship. Moving forward, he was on board with a fully established "No dating" policy amongst the staff. I recognize this situation could have worked out differently, but based on the relationship I had with him and wanted to keep, my tactic worked. The ultimate lesson here is that I had to really think about what was the right thing to do in this specific situation, and also be ready to take a different, more hard-line approach had my 1st attempt been unsuccessful.

## Corporate and Personal Ethical Standards Pay Off

I was tasked with expanding our business into international countries. This involved traveling to several countries to meet with potential distributors, customers, and government officials. We needed to find new ways to grow and sustain our business. Additionally, several of our global business units were proactively advocating for product commercialization in these countries to promote their own revenue growth.

A few of the countries were viable commercial targets; however, one country presented some ethical challenges. Our corporate policy clearly states that we conduct business honestly and fairly. Specifically, we do not condone practices that unduly influence purchasing decisions such as kick-backs or payments. For one country that I visited, these practices were the accepted norm. It was simply the way things were done there.

The discussions were going well in one potential customer engagement. At one point, a high-ranking government official entered the room, whispered to one of their staff and left. It was very subtle, but I noticed a change in the demeanor of the distributor that coordinated the meeting. When I asked him about it after the meeting, he shared that the government official was corrupt, and he wouldn't allow the deal to go through without his cut.

Given the nature of business partner relationships, it is easy enough to turn a blind eye and allow the distributors to manage all the deals using the local business practices without ever implicating our company. Our only options included commercially releasing our products in these countries, forgoing commercial release in these countries, or conditionally commercially releasing in these countries. Based on our policies and corporate standards, I recommended that we not commercialize in the countries with standard kickback practices because it was in conflict with our corporate values.

We ended up not doing business in these countries, and we were still able to grow our business in other ways and countries that did not conflict with our corporate values. Different cultures are hard to understand without actually experiencing them. Because others did not experience it first hand, I had to spend a lot of time justifying my decision. There was a lot of pressure from others hungry for the business to find ways of working around the problem. I really had to work hard to convince others to walk away from the business in these countries.

Biggest lessons? I realized that I had been very naïve and trusting. It taught me trust less and to pay much closer attention to nuances and details. If you are going to be in business at any level, you have to consider the long term. Honesty, integrity, and compassion are fundamental. Once you slip, everything is questionable.

## Friends Don't Push Their Agenda on Other Friends

As a manager, I was once faced with a decision to hire an internal friend who was significantly less qualified than others for a position. I wanted to keep the integrity of the current team but didn't want to lose a friend. I chose to hire a more qualified individual. I lost a "friend" but I kept the integrity of the team. I learned that a true friend would not have put me or the team in this position to begin with. A person is not your friend if they ask you to lower your integrity and attempt to put you in a position where a choice can create ill will toward each other.

**Group Caught In Skinny Dipping Incident**

I was in a senior leadership role working for a public relations unit that traveled extensively. The organization consisted of about a hundred personnel. I was directly responsible for thirty-six team members. My group included both junior and senior members of the organization. I had close friendships with some of these team members. Personal standards of conduct were enforced with the utmost attention. They were taken very seriously as the organization had contact with the public on a daily basis.

An incident occurred on one of our travels that involved six people, including four of my team. One of my team members was a leader within the organization and a personal friend of mine. Word of misconduct related to a swimming incident started to circulate throughout the organization after it was discovered that the police had been called due to reports of inappropriate behavior on the beach outside our hotel.

I had been informed of the incident by another person in the organization and knew I had an ethical obligation to investigate the situation. If these rumors proved to be true and the incident leaked to the public having not been addressed, this could cause significant damage to the public relations geared mission of the organization. Additionally, it was clear that my team members had violated our organization's personal conduct standards.

I could have ignored the rumor and pretend I had never heard about the situation, take the rumor to my senior leaders to start an investigation or, try to take care of the problem at the lowest possible level and attempt to resolve internally before moving forward. I decided to confront the leader who was rumored to have been involved to gain a clearer picture of the police incident. When questioned, he denied involvement and stated that there was no truth to any of the rumors circulating throughout the organization.

Because this was in direct contradiction to the information that I had gathered, I knew I had to do the honest thing and take the situation to my senior leaders for investigation. We conducted a full internal investigation and all parties involved were found guilty of personal conduct violations. The junior personnel were given the lightest punishments while the senior leader involved received the most severe discipline.

The main thing I learned from this situation was the importance of maintaining one's honesty and integrity when faced with difficult ethical situations in the work place.

**Everything Comes Back To Honesty And Integrity**

I previously worked at a company who issued reward 'stickers' for our marketing programs. Generally speaking, for every X dollar spent on account with us, Y research stickers were issued and these stickers could be used to receive rewards in the form of gifts. Based on their use of stickers to receive a rather large number of gifts, it soon became clear that ABC Corporation was one of our top accounts. However, I was concerned that the company was potentially giving away rewards for products not actually purchased.

After some investigation, I found that the sales person was stealing stickers from our shipping department and either sending them to the account in question or simply dropping them off when visiting the account. As my duties involved collecting the research stickers from accounts, one day I received over 30 sheets of stickers (100 stickers per sheet!) from one particular account – which seemed way too much even though it was our "top account".

After I pulled the sales history in order to match the dollar amounts with stickers issued, it was clear there was a huge discrepancy. I decided to inform management.

The sales person in question was fired – I was told that this was only one of a number of "contributing factors".

Ultimately, I am a bit disappointed as a number of people would have had to be involved for this scheme to be effective and none of those people were ever, to my knowledge, held accountable. Do everything with honesty and integrity – even if it is harder, because in the end, everything that goes around comes around.

## Using Company Time For Personal Matters

I was the office manager of a small start-up. The CEO was using company resources to take care of non-company related issues. She asked me to handle financial problems from a previous business venture including fielding calls from collection agencies! I felt this was unprofessional and a poor use of my time.

As a low-level employee I felt uncomfortable saying "no" to the company CEO. To complicate matters, I was both the office manager and the human resources manager. This left me without an avenue to lodge a complaint. The only option was to directly confront the CEO or to simply not react at all. After a good deal of deliberation, I decided to confront the CEO to let her know I was uncomfortable conducting her personal matters during business hours. I made it clear that she had hired me to help organize her business, create business processes, and establish rules and norms for employee management. I let her know that going forward, I would only conduct business related to those tasks.

Unfortunately, things did not turn out well. I confronted the CEO and she made it clear that she expected that the office manager would take care of these issues. As a result, I started looking for other jobs and we eventually parted ways (mostly amicably).

Move on if you are uncomfortable with the job requirements. There are other jobs out there which will not require you to compromise your morals. First, attempt to fix the situation, but sometimes the best option is to walk away.

## Don't Discount Your Ethics

I was a college student working part-time for a department store in a small town. The townspeople were all familiar with each other – the town had a very close knit community. Most of the students at the university knew each other or are familiar with their fellow students. After I started working at the department store, it became apparent that some employees were giving discounts or deals on items sold to their friends or popular classmates.

One day, Lisa, a popular student from town, came into the store. Lisa was older and was respected in the community and on campus. She came to my register with a basket of items including two expensive blouses. She pulled the blouses out of her basket, handing them to me, she said "It's so great that these are on sale today for 50% off. That's why I love this store and the people who work here."

When I rang up the blouses, they were not on sale, and I told her that. Lisa tried to convince me that I should ring the more expensive items up using the product code for a much cheaper item. She said it happens all the time and that it was no big deal. I wasn't going to be in that job for much longer anyway so what did I care?

I could have rung up the items at the incorrect price, tell her no and ring up the items at the regular price, or report the situation to my manager. I was really taken aback that this person I saw every day, and had no reason to suspect anything but good things of, was asking me to commit a crime. Her sales pitch was strong and I was a naïve 21-year-old. I was tempted to do it just to get this awkward situation over with.

In the end, I told her that I wasn't comfortable with what she'd asked. In fact, I had to tell her a few times. My coworkers were grateful and backed me on the decision. They had not wanted to give out the discounts either, but felt intimidated by the older students.

Be wary of people using friendliness as a technique for influence and not fall into a trap of doing something that violates your morals or jeopardizes your personal career for a better social status. Personal ethics and integrity are something to hold above the spheres of influence. Trust your gut and if something feels off take time to think about what you are doing. Usually standing up for your values will lead to others also coming out and standing up for theirs as well. Leading by example can be a very influential tool.

## You are in Agreement If You Don't Speak Up

I was once involved on an internal work committee which oversaw animal welfare. The committee was made up of both internal and external company members. The committee worked as a democracy in which the majority rules, but everyone had the opportunity to voice their concerns or opinions. At one meeting, an incident was brought up in which one member who was also a facility manager did not agree on a decision that was made by the committee.

He decided to get upper management involved to overturn the decision. The committee was supposed to be impartial to management. However, outsiders were brought in to try to influence the committee's decision.

I could have let upper management influence the committee and overturn the decision that was made to accommodate this facility manager, or I could have called out the facility manager for unethical behavior. Ultimately, I decided to voice my opinion about the situation to both upper management as well as to the committee. I wanted to make sure that all members saw the ramifications of the situation.

As a result, management declined to participate, as the committee is a regulatory body that is standalone from regular company operations. The facility manager was warned about his behavior. Feelings were hurt and attitudes were negative from the facility manager and the minority of the committee. However, the majority of the committee were happy with the outcome.

It's all about character. Promotions, referrals, and friendships are all based on one's character. No, we are not all perfect, but what truly matters is that we all have good intentions and our characters are the attribute by which we are judged.

## Keep Your Friends Close and Data Vendors Closer

As background, I have to say that the financial industry has evolved significantly in the last few years from a standpoint of ethics and legal framework. There are very few issues left that are unethical but legal. Ever since the financial crises, there is even more focus on ethics and legal framework, both in terms of regulatory or internal.

For example, 10 years ago, I could sell an investment product to a customer without disclosing that the investment sponsor pays me a commission. Clearly, it was a conflict of interest, but no one really made it compulsory to disclose. It was left to each salesperson. Of course, now, it is a law and full disclosure is essential as part of customer information law.

In that context, I would say that ethical situations can very quickly become legal or reputational risks. Large financial institutions today have very little tolerance for these risks, and hence, this really becomes a question of good risk management. Therefore controls, processes and validation are essential. This is what takes good leadership today.

Let me give you an example. A few months ago, we decided to launch a new investment product. It was a specialized investment product for a niche segment. We realized there was little competition in that segment, and that the margins were very high. Like we do for all our investment products, we used an external data vendor, like an outsourcing company, to manage the systems and database related to the product. We had a six month launch time frame, and executive management was very keen on meeting this deadline.

Very soon into the process, we realized that our largest competitor also uses the same vendor for a very comparable product. We looked around, and we could not find a quick replacement for this vendor or try to process them in-house. Even if we did, the costs and transition time was very high. This would make the product economically unviable and we could not meet the deadline set by the management.

This was an ethical issue at two levels: we were using the services of a third party to rely on a key product launch, and they were having to deal with two product owners competing for the same segment. Naturally, there was hesitation all around, and the ethical, legal and reputational risks were high. The options were very limited. We could either a) postpone the launch until we found another service provider, b) try to do that data processing in house, or c) work with the existing provider, but ensure we could address all the ethical issues for both of us.

Postponing the product launch was briefly considered, but it became clear that it would embarrass the senior management, who had publicly announced the plan to launch the new product. As a publicly traded company, that would not have helped our image or stock price! Hence, we had to stick to the commitment made.

We also looked at bringing the processing and data in-house, but at the time we did not have the staff and the resources to do this as efficiently as we would have liked. The turnaround time was also key, and unless we brought over an entire team from our vendor, this would not have been possible. Also, hiring people (or temps) with the level of skills needed was considered very unlikely.

We decided to go with the current vendor. But for that to work, we needed to create an ethics and legal risk team, which was led by me. The team composed of business, systems and legal experts in both firms and the idea was to ensure that there was full transparency and auditing of the data stored in the vendor. We also agreed to have the data audited periodically by an external consultant. The consultant would then give us rating reports, which would determine the frequency and costs of future audit.

We paid for the initial audit, but the onus was kept on the vendor for future audits. Things turned out better than expected. The cost of service was higher than what we planned due to the costs of the audit. However, that was money well spent. As mentioned earlier on, transparency is critical when dealing with ethical dilemmas.

In this case, we saw the external data auditors report as a key reference document to build on mutual trust. There were issues in the first audit report that needed to be fixed. Part of those costs came back to us. After the second iteration, the systems were fully insulated and we had confidence that we could go ahead with the product launch. There was some delay in the whole process, and the final launch deadline had to be pushed back.

Again, in the context of reputational and ethical risks, we wanted to get it right the first time. There are always business and profitability priorities, but risk management is always the foremost priority. This was always clear to me earlier on, but it was a new learning for some in my team.

It really struck me that 'ethical leadership' in this industry is closely linked to management of people, transparency and mutual protection. For example, while we as a financial institution want to be ethical and truthful, it is equally likely that a data vendor who works with the industry is equally motivated, even though they aren't regulated as we are. They do that to protect their future clients from such conflict of interests. In short, the responsibility lies with everyone.

**Your Good Name is Worth More Than Money**

When my husband's aunt died, his two nephews and niece sued the estate for a share of the inheritance. My husband and I and the other heirs were brought into arbitration to settle the matter. The nephews and niece openly lied about multiple incidents regarding the intentions of the estate. I was even more embarrassed for them than angry at them. What I took away from this situation is that when you die, what's left on earth of you is your good name.

Since it was our word against theirs, the only option was to give in, it was only money. They are family, not good family. Regardless, guilt tends to drive people away. The lawyers who were involved in the arbitration were shaking their heads because the truth was so obvious to everyone but the nephews and the niece. These people were family and somewhere along the line they were raised to act like that. It was just money, so we decided to give in.

To this day, we have never heard from them again. I have no idea if they were pleased with the result of their lawsuit. I was sad for my husband as the arbitration really hurt his feelings, but in the end this event didn't make an impact on our lives. To me money really isn't that important. I earn what I can and that's enough. I refuse to be a cheat or a liar over money.

## Follow Through On Your Commitments

I was friends with two coworkers when they both quit without notice. They both had told me about it ahead of time. I knew that this would hurt the store, the partners, and our customers, but they were my friends so I didn't know what to do. I could have told our manager, and she could have tried to get things covered, but I would have looked like a disloyal friend. I also could have tried to get them to change their minds; to be less selfish about the situation. It was difficult for the rest of us who stayed with the company to try and cover their slack. It totally changed my outlook on being close friends with people at work and what the boundaries were.

Through this experience, I realized I didn't want to be friends with people that would make those kinds of choices. I stopped associating with them after that. Make sure you follow through on your commitments. You may not like it, but it's not just about you.

**Honesty And Standing Your Ground With Employees**

I was recently promoted to sales manager, and one of my best salesman confronted me one Monday. He said a close personal mentor of his had unexpectedly passed away, and it hit him hard. He seemed very upset. He asked if he could take off a couple days next week for bereavement and so he could attend the funeral in Florida. Although it wasn't an immediate family member, I granted him permission to take off the remainder of the week.

I'm also connected to this person on social media. Later that Thursday, I saw a picture posted of him at a particular music festival with some friends. One of the friends was another one of my salesman, who requested the time off to for vacation, and I granted it. After doing further research, it was obvious to me this salesman lied in order to get time off. I later checked to see if all of his used vacation time was up, because I wanted to see if that was an incentive for him to lie about the death. It was true.

I could report this to my manager and HR, and at worst he could have been terminated. Or, I could keep him on board, because he was my best salesman, and I was trying to prove myself to management. I could keep this to myself and no one would find out. I took a couple weeks to think about it. I was afraid to confront this person, because it was my first leadership role and I wasn't used to confrontation. I ended up calling him into my office and I brought up the information I found. I emphasized that I wasn't suspicious of you, but that the evidence fell in my hands. He confessed and told me that this music festival was one of his lifelong dreams to attend. I told him I was obligated to report this to HR.

HR reprimanded him, and really did not impose a penalty. Essentially, he got away with it. It left a sour taste in my mouth, but it was out of my control. I could tell this employee was shaken up though. I did get positive recognition from my superiors, who told me the last manager did not deal with one particular unethical issue the way I did.

As a new manager, set an example to your employees and your superiors early. Trust your judgment. If you let things go, more dilemmas will likely happen and you'll lose control.

## If You Always Tell the Truth, You Don't Have to Remember Your Story

I was in a political position where I was in charge of a bidding process for a large project. One of the contractors offered me a bribe in exchange for competitors' bid information so they could win the contract. It was significant because it wouldn't be fair and it would be dishonest.

I could have taken the bribe. I probably could have escaped conviction and my family could have used the money at the time. I also had the option to turn down the bribe and conduct a fair bidding process. I turned down the bribe in a face-to-face meeting with the contractor. I told the contractor that it would be wrong and unethical to provide that information in a sealed bid process. I realized I couldn't live with a lie hanging over my head for the rest of my life. I felt good and proud of myself. If you stray from the path just once, chances are you'll go down the wrong path and do it again digging yourself a deeper and deeper hole.

Always be truthful and do what you feel is right. Having a conscience and moral fiber is a great thing. Not wanting a guilty feeling is a good character trait to have. Be honest in all your dealings. If you always tell the truth, you don't have to remember your story.

**Integrity Overcomes Evil**

Years ago, I was a CFO for a public utility and my mentor was the CEO at the time. During this time, there was a company executive that would routinely falsify and inflate his expense report, then bring it to me to pay. I felt terribly uncomfortable with this situation and I made the CEO aware of what was going on. There were a lot of variables. It was fairly early in my career, the CEO had not been in his very position long, and several members of the Board of Directors had close, personal relationships with this executive.

The CEO was faced with three difficult options; let it go by turning a 'blind eye', just give the executive a slap on the wrist or the third option, terminate him and press charges. I found an even deeper respect for my CEO for the decision he made. The CEO chose to terminate the executive and press charges, knowing that it would potentially end the executive's professional career. After the executive was terminated by the CEO, formal charges were pressed and he was ordered by the courts to pay restitution but was never sent to jail. Essentially, his professional career was ended.

The incident sent a message to the rest of the company. If executives were not immune to being brought to justice, no one else would be either. The board members that were friends of the executive were eventually rotated off of the board. Another good thing that happened as a result of this event was that the culture of the company began to change, for the better.

Lessons learned? Nothing is more important than integrity. You only have one chance to lose integrity. Once it's lost, you will never get it back. It's never about you. Always do what is right for the company and stick to your principles.

## Keep Ethical Considerations in Mind When Making Decisions

An employee at our consulting firm was billing extra time for a project he was working on with a client. This was significant because it could hurt our reputation as a small consulting agency, and it is unethical to bill for time that was not spent working on a project. We could either fire the employee, or reprimand and re-train the employee.

We ended up firing the employee as this was not the only performance issue; rather this issue was the straw that broke the camel's back. We put another employee on the project and retrained our employee consultants about proper billing practices. The project was still successful with the new consultant and the rest of the employees were more aware of the strict rules when it comes to billing for time on a project.

Some employees don't consider the ethical implications when it comes to their actions. No one might have ever noticed that the employee was billing for extra time and for items outside of the project scope. The employee may also have felt like it wasn't exactly an unethical thing to do. Retraining out consultants on ethical implications of their actions was a positive outcome.

If you don't live your life with honesty and integrity, even if no one finds out, it will eat away at you. If it ever gets to the point where it doesn't bother you anymore, then you have some real problems. To avoid this, develop your values and try to live your life by abiding to them.

## Widow Stays Devoted To Husband

In the early 1980's, my parents were driving on a major highway. A driver was speeding and changing lanes. That driver clipped the rear bumper of my parent's car. My father lost control, the car became airborne, crossed the center divider and collided with a third car. That driver of the third car died and my mother sustained a leg fracture. The young man that was speeding had no car insurance. My mother faced an ethical dilemma when the lawyer told her that in order to collect insurance she would need to say that my father was responsible for the accident (my father was deceased at the time that the insurance board met with my mother and her lawyer.) My mother could lie and collect a substantial sum or tell the truth and receive $10,000.

She told the truth when asked and stated that the uninsured reckless driver caused the accident. In her heart, she could not blame my father for something he did not do. She received only the $10,000. The lawyer's fee took a big bite of that. My mother had to cover all additional costs out of her own pocket and not receive any compensation for her pain and suffering. I learned that preserving one's integrity may be more important than money to honest people. You have to live with your decisions. When you make the right decision, your mind and your heart meet at your gut.

## Give Credit Where Credit Is Due

While I was working with a travel and hospitality client for the project of joint venture integration, one of my coworkers had created one complete module related to graphical user interface in the processing system for one of the travel groups. According to the schedule, she was supposed to give an interactive presentation regarding the changes to all the key stakeholders in a conference, and was asked to take the business signoff. So she prepared one presentation and one prototype.

Unfortunately, just two days before the presentation, she became ill and handed over the presentation and the prototype to the manager. Because this sign-off was one critical phase of the requirement gathering stage, and I was working as the scrum master of whole joint-venture delivery, the onshore manager asked me to take charge. I presented the prototype and discussed all the possible requirement scenarios. I successfully documented the signed off requirements and received the client champion award for the best prototype customization of application and brainstorming session. I received many appreciations from client as well as the client management. Of course, the actual contribution was not mine.

I had two options, either to take the credit for her work and take all the appreciation and awards or to announce that her contribution was the real effort behind this joint venture integration module. I was not comfortable with these appreciations because the major effort for this session was not mine: it was my teammate's hard work.

I informed my delivery manager about the real effort behind this award. Consequently, the award was re-awarded to both of us. This incident helped me understand that it is important to treat everyone fairly. This situation helped me think beyond a personal level. I thought about my responsibilities as a professional and my responsibilities towards my colleagues. I realized that one should serve her organization with integrity. I recognized that a behavior based on equity, justice, and a sense of obligation to others can lead to good long term collaboration.

## Personal vs. Professional: Keep Them Separate

During my time at a manufacturing company, I was a popular HR Director among my colleagues. I tried my best to be friendly and personable, yet straightforward with my job and its requirements. One thing I enjoyed about this position was that I was close to many of my employees. I had a personal relationship with one of my employees, Frank, and with his family as well. Frank was not only a friendly person who did his job well, he was also very likeable among many of our colleagues. Many times I would give Frank a ride home from work when his car would not work, and I noticed many other employees would reach out to help Frank in their own ways.

As nice of a person as Frank was, he unfortunately had a substance abuse problem that affected his work. Frank was a member of our company's substance abuse program. While he had previously recovered and completed the program, he had regressed and was once again part of the substance abuse program. Part of our company program was random tests would be administered by us at any time we felt necessary. This policy was an agreement between the Company and the Union, so Frank had proper notification that this may occur. One of these random tests ultimately led to Frank failing, and per company policy, he had to be terminated.

Legally, for all parties involved, this was a very clear cut case. As previously stated, Frank had been properly notified, so failing the test meant he had to be terminated. This policy was clearly outlined in our company's contract with the union, so there was no way for Frank or the union to file a grievance. This should have been a very simple case that led to an employee's termination, however, my own emotions and ethics complicated the situation.

I had no other option but to follow the company's policy and procedures, so as the Human Resources Director I was in the position to terminate my friend. Perhaps the most difficult part of the termination was knowing he was the only provider for his 6 children. While I reminded myself, I had no other option at this point, I still found it very difficult to deliver the news to Frank.

I scheduled a meeting with Frank to discuss his termination, however all parties involved knew beforehand the meeting outcome. Frank tried to give me some desserts his wife had made for me several times prior to the meeting. Knowing Frank would want to discuss other options, I decided not to meet with him beforehand. During the meeting, the termination letter was presented and received as you might expect. Frank broke down in tears, and while my demeanor remained professional, knowing his situation I was very conflicted on the inside. Having no car, Frank could not even drive home after the meeting, therefore a fellow employee drove him home on that last day.

As professionals, you are often going to be required to make decisions or deliver news to employees that are uncomfortable and perhaps make you unlikable. During these inevitable scenarios, I would like to emphasize that in delivering tough news, you must always present that information with compassion, honesty, respect, firmness, and dignity. During my situation with Frank, I surely tried to do this, despite feeling such turmoil inside. A key, yet seemingly unspoken attribute among Human Resource professionals is our desire and willingness to help people. In such a case like this, and even in life you should always try to remember, no matter how much you want to help someone, they must be willing to help themselves.

## Just Say No

When I was out of law school, I was working for a downtown law firm and putting in a ton of hours. That sounds cliché, right? At the time I had a roommate in a great old converted service house downtown. It was a killer location, great house, tons of room and the rent was a deal, but still not easy to make. The roommate situation was good because we had been friends and worked together in the past and there was very little drama.

Regardless, the fact that I was at the firm most of the time put me out of touch with what was going on with my roommate. In the span of about 3 months, she went from dating some guy who I thought was sort of shady, to being in a drug-heavy bad situation. Beyond being concerned about her downward spiral and her health, I was stuck paying the rent solo for a few months in a row while I heard from her that she'd cover her rent.

I had very little I could do. I tried talking to her and talking to our shared friends. Neither had any impact on her. The cycle of confronting her, then being told that she'd turn it around, then that not happening proved too much. I finally got so tired of it that I contacted our landlord and had her taken off the lease and evicted her.

Her last day on the lease was a Saturday-her move out day. It came and went. She didn't show up. I stayed home that whole day to help move boxes or whatever needed to happen. Nothing. So I was faced with a key decision: Do I contact the police or do something else? I decided to contact her parents. This was sort of ridiculous to call a 28 year old's parents, but when I thought more, these were people who undoubtedly care about her. I'd met them once. I still had a rough feeling that I was telling on her or tattling or just breaching some sort of trust. Either way, I thought it was the right thing to do with very few options.

It took me a bit to find their number, but when I reached them, I was pretty straightforward and honest about the situation. I didn't shy away from telling them that I believed that their daughter had a drug problem and was in a very bad relationship that was enabling her bad decision making. I did then and still believe that she is at fault, too. I emphasized, however that the path she chose with this situation was not like the person I knew. Either way, I talked to them and they said they were leaving Charlotte, her hometown, and driving to my house immediately.

They got to town, waited for her to come home and then put her in the car and took her home. They got her admitted into a rehabilitation program and even squared up with me on the back rent. In the end, she turned it around, is married, has a son and has her life on track. I'm glad I did it. Looking back, it was an easy decision, to do what's right for her, but it was a tough decision at the time.

I learned that you have to do what you think is right. I knew all along that I wasn't really concerned about the rent. I mean, that was a real concern financially, but I didn't like to see a friend go downhill like that. Do the right thing even when it's challenging.

**Surround Yourself With Ethical Friends**

I was with my friends (very smart and savvy individuals) the night before an important neuroscience test. The subject was definitely not an easy one and we were all unsure of ourselves. As we continued to study into the wee hours of the night, one friend was struggling with the material more than the rest of us. We were a multi-year group with large differences in knowledge. I watched as Mary and Liz had a private conversation (which I happened to overhear) about how stressed Liz was and how she was considering cheating by writing notes and answers on the label of her water bottle. I was curious as to what Mary was going to tell her to do.

We've all been taught that cheating is wrong, that sentiment is even echoed in the school honor code and the syllabus for the class. We were at a rigorous undergraduate institute that highly discouraged cheating and the consequences were dire. Now why are these two important? They were seniors to my sophomore status and I looked up to both of them as leaders in our sorority. They were also two of my closest friends and they were roommates. Their lives were so entwined it was interested to watch how Mary would handle the situation and the impact on their relationship. I sat and watched and listened and here is what Mary did.

She used her relationship with Liz to help sway her in the ethically (no cheating) correct decision. She advised Liz to study as much as she could take the test and then approach the teacher asking for extra help after Liz said she was having trouble grasping the material and just needed more time. It was a rational approach and one that worked well in the long and short term.

Liz didn't do well on the test but learned a valuable lesson about approaching a teacher and asking for help. She then improved her scores in the future and actually ended up learning more about neuroscience than she would have. Mary learned that not necessarily telling her friend what she should do worked wonders, and it didn't strain their relationship at all. I saw this as an organic growth opportunity and applied those principles to the rest of my leadership roles.

## *A Parting Thought*

"You have to be prepared to suffer negative consequences in upholding integrity and ethics. You cannot allow personal suffering to deter you from doing the right thing. It involves a great deal of risk-sometimes, life changing risk-and these are the things you cannot list on your resume. These things have to be a part of your soul and not just words. They have to be more important to you than your creature comforts. If not, it will be too easy to back away."

~From an anonymous
every day values based leader

## *List of Contributors*

Thanks to the many contributors from NC State's Poole College of Management who interviewed everyday values based leaders. We're confident they are now practicing the ethical lessons in their chosen fields.

## BSBA Contributors

Laura Elizabeth Allen
Lauren Michele Anderson
Yachu Baranski
Armin Jamaal Barkley
Emily Jane Beckman
Kelsey Elizabeth Benson
Kelsey Lee Boggs
Jessica D (Nikki) Boyd
Rachel Christine Brame
Kaitlyn Rose (Katie) Brinn
Christopher Franklin Brinn
Alyson M Brown
Michael Brandon Cornell
Dominic Prospero DeLizza III
Emily Alexandra DeZubay
Casey Laine Dorsett
Hamilton A Dubois
Emma Katherine Earwood
Zachary H Fitzgerald
Yasser Khaled Anwar Ghadiry
Mallory Allyson Holtz
Sarah Ellen Hooks
Chelsea Paige Hunt
Joy Christiana Jackson
Christin P James
Kellie Eileen Janes
Beth Johnson
Margaret Grace Kenney
Binita Lamdari
Shanice Danielle Leaks
Jordan Lewis
Sarah R Lewis
Katie Lynn Lewis
Elizabeth Lor
Tara Jane Lucas
Adan Maldonado Nolasco
Erin Elizabeth McInerny
Ashley Christine Mentzer
Elizabeth M (Liz) Morgan
Emily Katherine Murphy
Lindsay Brooke Nadell
Madison Ann Ott
Anna Marie Owens
Chandler Nichole Pearce
Myah N Perry
Kyle Martin Phares
Susannah L (Susie) Raichle
Simone Phyllis Ramdeen
Ashley N Ranaudo
Joseph Glenn Reynolds
Sydney Alexandra Shackelford
Suhani Pragnesh Shah
Molly Rebecca Sink
Joseph Garrett Squires
Jennifer Jeanne Swanson
James Adrian (Adrian) Taylor

Kate McKinley Tripp

Joseph Carlton (Joe) Trotter

Victoria Christian Tsitouris

Arlan C Wallace

Kayla Diane Ward

Mary Catherine Webb

Amanda Lauren Wildt

Rebekah Leanne Williams

Melody Sue Woodyard

## MBA Contributors

Mahomet Accilien
Elizabeth Trimble Adams
Himanshu Agrawal
Brian William Anderson
Justin Byron Angel
Samuel Rubin Ansel
Kristin Ardillo
Atrin Assa
Lu Yin Athnos
Brian Patrick Babcock
Mia Denise Bailey
Ilaria Ballan
Garima Bansal
Michael Omax Barr
Aaron Ted Beddingfield
Lenson Leroy Bellamy III
William Arthur Bernholz
Kenneth Edward Biryla
Katina M Blue
Elizabeth Thompson Bowen
Matthew Ignatius Boyle III
Ashley Raper Bristow
Brian Paul Brown
Charles Douglas Bull
Roger Vincent Burns
Erin Elizabeth Burns
John James Calvert
Edward Thomas Campbell III
Rolando J Carrillo
Stephanie Rains Carter
Sean M Carter
Robert Glenn Caudle
Vidyalakshmi Chandramohan
Roger Tsokang Chang
Cynthia Szu-Chen Chou
Chad Richard Clapp
Craig James Comito
Kristy N Craig
Charles Grant Culbertson Jr
Katherine Elaine Curtis
Joshua Benjamin Dalton
Candace Elyse Daniels
Harry Leon Davis
Michelle L. Davis
Izzay Roy Denney
Jeffrey Despain
Ricardo Andres DiFranco
Chris Michael Dodson
Arthur Francis Doucette
Josiah Mark Drewry
Ryan Eades
Bryan Christopher Earnhardt
Meredith Ahles Elrod
Taisir El-Souessi
Nathan Daniel Evans
Tiera Michelle Fann
Samuel Gardner Fasola

Amie Boes Fish
Alex Hill Flora
John Marshall Fowle Jr
Jason Thomas Gauthier
Hunter Lee Gay
Theresa Gibson
Clay William Giese
Kimberly Renne Gonzalez
Cory Jamal Gray
Kyle Hutchinson Green
Amanda Noel Gregory
Austin Reid Grimes
Pratap Reddy Gudur
Taylor Anderson Hale
Eric Bruce Harper
Steven Christopher Harpham
Andrea Lauren Hauser
Jason David Heffernan
Mark Stephen Henderson
Nicklaus Hetfeld
Luke P High
Kathryn Ann Hill
Dawn Holden
Kayla Nicole Horst
Patrick Gordon Horst
Daniel Stafford Howarth
Leo Foster Howell
Jennifer Erin Huffman
Rachel E Huffman
Philip Monroe Hurst
John Andrew Isenhour
Lauren Taylor James
Nancy Jawabreh
Concepcion Jimenez-Gonzalez
Kurleen Khavia John
Katherine L Jones
Colleen Kenney Jordan
Kapila Kaushik
Christine Marie Keating
Michael Denis Keating
Christine Marie Keating
Michael Denis Keating
Kristina Marie Kennard
Kelly Ashlinn Kiger
Junghun Kim
Peter Hasal Klavik
Katherine Kleinknecht
Corrina Maria Knight
John Aaron Kohler
Albert Leon Kok
Kyle Eric Kras
Krutika Kutty
Jonathan M Lamb
Anna Smith Lambert
Lei Lan
Lili Liu
John Stratton Lobdell
Xiaoming Lu

Pritesh Paritosh Majmundar
Kenneth Brandon Majoros
Kimberly Michelle Mangum
Kristen Martin
Allison Christine McFadden
Christopher Thomas Meade
Blake Edward Miller
Catherine Scott Mitchell
Karla Yudy Molero Callirgos
Tristan Charles Moore
Jean-Carroll Velazquez Moseley
Amy Bowman Mull
Sean Christopher Munday
Holly Marie Munn
Daniel Robert Murdough
Tiffany Harness Nail
Marilyn Hazard Nolte
Lisa Michelle O'Hal
Heather Aileen O'Keefe
Ozgun Oral
Hayley Ward Osmon
Darshana Sanjeev Paithankar
Brian Keith Parnell
Matthew John Petschauer
Ambica Pilli
Natasha Theresa Pinto
Jonathan David Powell
Dustin Ryan Prescott
Vicki McBride Radcliffe
Justin Sean Radloff
Donovan Robinson Ragsdale
Shyam Ram
Nick Ramirez
Gary Wayne Ray
Gary Wayne Ray
Franziska Verena Schmidt
Margaret Ellen (Meg) Schneider
Iris Nathalie Schonenberg
William Joseph Scott
Glenn Liss Setliff
Steven Louis Shaffer
Jinang Shah
Nimil Simon
Nadine Elizabeth Smith
Angela Marie Stoehr
Sophia Yue Su
Bryan Michael Sulier
Jayanthi S Suryanarayanan
Neha Shantaram Suryavanshi
Kaitlin Mckinney Szulik
Warner Lewis Tabb
Robert Joseph Terranova
Harry Raymond (Ray) Tidaback
Chirag Vinodkumar Tilva
Sandra Ann Tompkins
Daniel Christopher Toton
Janelle Devonne Tracy
Alicia Thi Tran

Derrell Jamison (Jamison) Vann
Grant Patrick Vick
Christopher Walter Voss
Devon Ashley Glick Wadsworth
Rodney Alan Walker
Kelly Ferguson Walton
Jamison Blake Ward
Bradley La Mont Webster
Richard James Weiland
Edward Terrell (Ted) Werner
William Phillip White
Zachary Christopher White
Jared Paul Whitehead
Michael Drew (Drew) Widman
Jennifer Renee Wiles
Paul Brooks Williams
Virginia Ann Willis
Michael Christopher Wires
Jeffrey Jared Wright
Christina Helen Wunsch
Fei Yao

## *About the Editors and the Cover Designer*

**Chris Hitch, Ph.D.** is a former Director of the General H. Hugh Shelton Leadership Center. He has over 30 years of leadership and management experience focusing on aligning strategy, leadership, and operations to drive solid business results. He has served in a wide variety of general management and senior level roles in the public and corporate sectors, primarily in startups, realignments, high growth, and turnaround organizations. Chris now serves as a Director of Custom Executive Development Programs at the University of North Carolina's Kenan-Flagler Business School. He consults and leads workshops on leadership, strategy, ethical decision making, and change. Chris and his wife, April, have two adult children, and one granddaughter.

**Beth Ritter** is a faculty member in the Poole College of Management at NC State University. She enjoys coaching current and future leaders in the areas of strategic human capital management and corporate social responsibility. Previously she worked for Fortune 500 companies in Human Resource leadership positions and now consults.

**Michael Saccavino**: Michael is a member of the Class of 2017 at UNC-Chapel Hill. He earned a double major in Economics and English. He served as lead editor on this project. He also was key in creating the marketing plan for the launch of this book.

**Madison Thompson** is a member of the Class of 2017 at NC State University. In her spare time, she enjoys creating art on numerous mediums, including wood, paper, canvas, metal, and digital art. She also enjoys immersing herself in nature, and draws much of her inspiration from the world around her. Madison enjoys spending time with her husband and the rest of her family. Madison cites the late Monty Oum of RoosterTeeth with giving her an attitude of positivity, with the simple message to "Keep moving forward."

CPSIA information can be obtained
at www.ICGtesting.com
Printed in the USA
BVOW06s0245050517
483306BV00014B/141/P